Frank S

A Life Worth Reading

Read it. Know it.™

Copyright © 2013 Higher Read, LLC.
PO Box 484, Sharon, MA 02067

Higher Read™ is a Limited Liability Company located in Sharon, Massachusetts
For more information about Higher Read™, visit www.HigherRead.com

All rights reserved, including the right to reproduce this book or portions thereof in any form whatsoever. For more information address Higher Read, LLC.
PO Box 484, Sharon, MA 02067.

First Higher Read™ paperback edition, January 2014

"Higher Read" and "Read it. Know it." are trademarks of Higher Read, LLC.

Cover design by Higher Read, LLC. Copyright © 2014 Higher Read, LLC. All rights reserved.

About Higher Read™

Take learning out of the ivory tower and into your hands. With Higher Read's™ original content, you have all the expertise of professionals in a convenient, accessible format. From organizing to learning about history to writing like a pro, continue your education with Higher Read's™ real-life guides and how-tos. Because doctors, lawyers, writers, and college professors contribute to the curriculum, you will read it and then you will know it.

We'd love to hear from you. If you have questions, comments, complaints, or compliments, please contact us at info@HigherRead.com or visit us online at www.HigherRead.com.

Foreword

Frank Sinatra, also known as The Voice, Ol' Blue Eyes, Leader of the Pack, and by countless other titles, was a man of many faces. Part mobster, part philanthropist, part political activist, and part civil rights leader, Frank participated in powerful institutions and movements that shaped America's history.

Although married four times and constantly surrounded by women, Frank was able to sing about loneliness with aching authenticity. He made teen girls swoon, beautiful women tremble, and grown men cry. Frank's intense personal dramas with women, the press, and the Mafia are intertwined with his musical career and the songs that will live on in the world's collective consciousness. Emerging from a poor immigrant neighborhood, Frank sang the country through massive changes and came to be the voice of urban America.

Frank Sinatra: A Life Worth Reading brings you all the successes, falls, and scandals that made Leader of the Pack a controversial public figure. An entertaining biography with special "in Brief" sections on the people and events that surrounded and shaped Frank's life, this book will give you the whole picture.

Table of Contents

Foreword..3
Chapter 1: Roots and Birth...7
   The Unification of Italy in Brief..12
   The Murder of David Hennessy in Brief...........................13
Chapter 2: Early Life and Family..14
   Prohibition in Brief..19
Chapter 3: Frank's Start as an Artist......................................21
   Bing Crosby in Brief..26
   The Great Depression in Brief...27
Chapter 4: Frank Sinatra, Rustic Cabin Boy and Lover...........28
Chapter 5: Frank Sinatra Makes the Big Time........................33
   Tommy Dorsey in Brief..39
   Buddy Rich in Brief...40
Chapter 6: The Attack of the Bobbysoxers.............................41
   Gene Kelly in Brief..46
Chapter 7: Frank Sinatra, Draft Dodger.................................47
   Lana Turner in Brief..51
Chapter 8: Frank Sinatra, Political Activist and Suspected Communist...52
   FDR in Brief..56
Chapter 9: Frank Sinatra, Mob Collaborator.........................57
   Lucky Luciano in Brief..65
Chapter 10: Frank Sinatra, Civil Rights Leader......................66
   Sammy Davis Jr. in Brief...71
Chapter 11: Frank and Lana...72
   Marilyn Maxwell in Brief...76
Chapter 12: The Beginning of the Fall...................................77
Chapter 13: Frank Sinatra, Mr. Gardner.................................80
   Montgomery Clift in Brief...88
Chapter 14: Frank Has a Little Help from His Friends............89
Chapter 15: Frank Sinatra, the Turbulent...............................93
   Zsa Zsa Gabor in Brief...102
Chapter 16: Frank Sinatra, Remade and Looking for Love....103
   Dean Martin in Brief...111
Chapter 17: The Rat Pack..112

Joey Bishop in Brief	116
Chapter 18: Frank and JFK	117
Peter Lawford in Brief	126
Chapter 19: Frank Sinatra, the Highest-Paid Man in Hollywood	127
Mia Farrow in Brief	132
Chapter 20: Frank in the 1960s	133
Chapter 21: Frank, the Retired Republican	138
Spiro Agnew in Brief	143
Chapter 22: Mrs. Barbara Sinatra	144
Zeppo Marx in Brief	149
Chapter 23: Frank Sinatra, Still Performing	150
Chapter 24: Death and Funeral	155
Afterword	158

Chapter 1: Roots and Birth

Biographers of Frank Sinatra commonly start his story by relating the history of his grandparents. Sinatra's roots, embedded in various regions in Italy and stretching over the Atlantic to the United States, played a key role in shaping his personality, goals, and opportunities.

Frank Sinatra's grandparents were not born into an Italy characterized by a uniform, harmonious cultural community. Italy had not been unified into one country until 1871, and individuals still clung to their regional identities, holding grudges and prejudices against persons from other regions. Frank's father's parents were born and raised in a rural area on the southern island of Sicily, where there was little education or chance for advancement. Frank's mother's parents belonged to educated families in the northern city of Genoa. Driven by poverty and the hope of finding a better life, both families joined the mass exodus from Europe that occurred between 1880 and the beginning of the First World War. Italians made up a significant percentage of the twenty-four million Europeans who left the continent. Most Italians settled in the United States while significant numbers migrated to Brazil and Argentina.

Both of Frank's grandparents' families settled in the immigrant slum of Hoboken, New Jersey. At that time, Americans looked with suspicion on the Italian immigrants' language and practices. Italians were declared "not white" and were targeted by the Ku Klux Klan and other bigots. Along with the Irish and the Jewish immigrants, they were excluded from mainstream society and viewed as an inferior ethnic minority. The Irish, who had been in the New York area longer, largely controlled the immigrant neighborhoods' government and social services.

Italian Americans quickly became plagued with another stereotype—that of being involved in brutal organized crime. In 1891, when a police chief in New Orleans was allegedly murdered by a group of Italian immigrants, the term and concept of the Mafia were introduced to the American public. The accused Italian immigrants were not convicted due to lack of evidence but were publicly lynched by a mob in New Orleans, a crime for which no one was punished. Ironically, this incident led many Italian Americans to believe that they could not count on the American criminal justice system, a belief that led some to seek the protection of the Mafia rather than face the corruption and blatant racism of American institutions.

Inside the Italian American community, a cultural battle was being waged between *la via vecchia* and *la via nuova*, or the old ways versus the new ways. The Italian immigrants expected their children both to act like Americans and to adhere to the cultural and moral norms of their Italian ancestors. Inevitably, the first generations of Italian

Americans were caught between these clashing expectations, with no guidance from their elders.

Antonino, or Marty, Sinatra, and Natalie, or Dolly, Garavente, who were to become Frank Sinatra's parents, grew up in the midst of this cultural clash in the immigrant slum of Hoboken, New Jersey. Marty's family came from a rural town in Sicily. He became a small-time boxer and laborer, fighting under the Irish name Marty O'Brien because an Italian-American wouldn't get any work in boxing at the time. He was a quiet young man who had received very little education. Dolly, whose family came from the northern city of Genoa, was outgoing, educated, and intelligent. She looked American, with her blond hair and light complexion. Against the wishes of both sets of parents, Dolly and Marty courted and married in Jersey City's City Hall on Valentine's Day, 1913. They later held a religious ceremony in their home to appease their parents.

Dolly and Marty moved into their own apartment on Monroe Street in Hoboken and got to work creating their American lives. Dolly got a job in a candy shop while Marty worked as a boilermaker in a shipyard. They were determined to have children and were dismayed when Dolly didn't become pregnant right away. In the spring of 1915, Dolly finally became pregnant.

On December 12, 1915, Frank Sinatra was born in the Monroe Street apartment. The birth was dangerous and traumatic to Dolly, who only weighed ninety pounds. Baby Frank weighed over thirteen pounds and presented in a breech, or sitting, position. Dolly was in agonizing labor for hours.

When the baby finally began to emerge from the birth canal, the doctor used forceps to hasten his exit, and Frank emerged blue and lifeless, his head and neck bleeding from the forceps. Dolly's mother, Rosa, a midwife by trade, shoved the baby under a faucet running cold water and thereby revived him to the surprise of the doctor, who had not believed that the baby would survive. Frank bore scars on his face and neck for the rest of his life as a result of the use of the forceps, and Dolly was left unable to have more children.

Frank's birth certificate recorded his name as "Frank Sinestro." The last name "Sinestro" was a clerical error, but the first name was Frank, not Francis after the baby's paternal grandfather Francesco. When he was in his twenties, Frank legally changed his name to Francis Albert Sinatra. He preferred that his friends call him Francis.

The Unification of Italy in Brief

The *Risorgimento*, as it was known, was an orchestrated movement to unite Italy both politically and culturally. Up until the *Risorgimento*, Italy was a geographical region (think of the Italian boot) comprised of Italian states ruled by other countries or dynasties.

Italian unification began in earnest in the middle of the nineteenth century. Many people were involved in the movement, including Giuseppe Mazzini and Giuseppe Garibaldi, but the final success of the movement in usually credited to Camillo di Cavour. Mazzini and Garibaldi attempted to unify Italy through popular uprisings. Their work helped grow the popularity of the cause and paved the way for Cavour.

Cavour was a count with political connections. He focused on diplomacy with the powers that held the Italian states. This tactic, along with Garibaldi's military leadership, ultimately succeeded. In 1861 the Italian states became the Kingdom of Italy. Over the next ten years, Italy would add to its territory to become Italy as we know it today.

The Murder of David Hennessy in Brief

In October of 1890, New Orleans police chief David Hennessy was killed outside his home. The murder resulted in the arrest of many Italians; most accounts report that dozens were taken into custody in a sweeping search for anyone who looked Italian. Of these, nineteen were detained for trial.

On March 13, the trial declared three of the men not guilty. There were various other verdicts for the rest, including mistrial and, in some cases, dismissing the charges altogether. The lack of evidence against the men is usually cited as the reason for these decisions. It is not surprising that the indiscriminate roundup of anyone of a certain ethnicity failed to provide evidence.

The next day, March 14, a mob stormed the prison and murdered eleven Italians. Some were clubbed, some shot, and some hanged. The media and public generally applauded the violent behavior of the mob. The media began to link Italians and Italian Americans to the Mafia, and the lynching and response almost created an international incident with Italy.

Chapter 2: Early Life and Family

Frank's position as an only child impacted him greatly in at least two ways. First, he had no other siblings with whom to share the experience of being a first-generation American in a community of Italians clinging to the Old Way. Furthermore, he was literally alone much of the time, which may have contributed to his ability to sing so authentically about loneliness later in life.

His mother Dolly was the dominant force in the family, ruling over both her husband and son. With her good looks and vivacious personality, Dolly was active in local politics and spent a great deal of time outside the house, frequently leaving Frank in the care of his grandparents.

Dolly also worked as a midwife and performed abortions at a time in which it was illegal to do so. She was convicted of performing these abortions at least twice. Dolly was very involved in the community and had learned all of the various dialects of Italian, making her a perfect candidate for a politician to bridge the gap between the Irish-controlled government and the various parts of the Italian immigrant community.

Frank's relationship with his mother remained complicated for most of his life. As a young mother, Dolly treated Frank as a piece of personal property, dressing him in girl's clothes (she had wanted a daughter) and dressing him up for pictures. She ignored his childhood fears and expected him to do whatever she wanted. She frequently punished him with beatings and outbursts. However, she was fiercely loyal to her son, always fighting her hardest to get him what he wanted and needed.

Frank's father Marty was a very quiet man. A boxer by trade, he seemed meek and mild until someone crossed him, at which time he would respond brutally with his fists. It is likely that he was illiterate. He was described as "a drinking man" and may have been an alcoholic. In the house, he bowed to Dolly's will.

The United States' entrance into World War I and the passing of Prohibition laws greatly affected the Sinatra family. Frank's father Marty was declared exempt from the draft due to his dependent family. Before Prohibition began, Hoboken's bars had been shut down, but the town had become a hotbed for the import of foreign liquor. After Prohibition, illegal bars and taverns proliferated, and Dolly opened her own under her husband's boxing name, calling the bar "Marty O'Brien's." Marty provided security to bootleggers, and the family prospered under the protection of the growing organized crime syndicate made up of Irish, Italian, and Jewish gangsters.

When Frank was entering his teenage years, the family moved up in the world, from the Monroe Street apartment to a nicer apartment in the German-Irish section of town. Dolly used her political connections to get Marty a job in the fire department, a position traditionally reserved for Irish immigrants. She and Marty kept the tavern open and lavished gifts on Frank. As a result, Frank was always dressed in nice clothes and given a significant allowance, which he used to buy his friends soda and other treats. Dolly bought Frank a car when he was fifteen, increasing his popularity with the other kids in town.

According to some sources, including Frank himself, Frank was frequently involved in street battles and was once beaten by the police for no reason other than his ethnicity. While Frank was certainly taught how to fight by his father, other sources say that Frank invented the story of a violent childhood in order to appear to be a tough guy when in reality he was a pampered, sheltered child. Whichever version of the story is true, Frank did not complete high school, dropping out soon after his freshman year. His father, who had not had the chance to receive education, was furious, but Dolly didn't believe that an education would make much of a difference in her son's chances of success.

The family continued to prosper and, in 1932, bought a house complete with a backyard. By 1931, Frank had met the person who would become his first wife, Nancy Barbato. Nancy was only fourteen when she met sixteen-year-old Frank Sinatra near their respective summer homes on the shore an hour to the south of Hoboken. Frank was attracted to Nancy's beauty and to the warmth and bustle of her family home. As opposed to his lonely, quiet childhood, Nancy had six siblings, and her large family welcomed Frank with hospitality. Frank loved the company and the noise.

By the time he was seventeen, Frank had already decided that he wanted out of Hoboken. He took the ferry into Manhattan as often as possible. Pictures show him gazing hungrily across the harbor toward New York City.

Prohibition in Brief

The Eighteenth Amendment to the U.S. Constitution was ratified in January 1919. It read:

Section 1

After one year from the ratification of this article the manufacture, sale, or transportation of intoxicating liquors within, the importation thereof into, or the exportation thereof from the United States and all territory subject to the jurisdiction thereof for beverage purposes is hereby prohibited.

Section 2

The Congress and the several states shall have concurrent power to enforce this article by appropriate legislation.

Section 3

This article shall be inoperative unless it shall have been ratified as an amendment to the Constitution by the legislatures of the several states, as provided in the Constitution, within seven years from the date of the submission hereof to the states by the Congress.

This amendment became law in January 1920. Prohibition was notoriously hard to enforce. People made their own liquor ("bootlegging"), and many profited from selling bootleg liquor. Bootlegging became linked with organized crime, including the notorious Al Capone.

In 1933 the Twenty-first amendment repealed the Eighteenth Amendment as follows:

Section 1

The eighteenth article of amendment to the Constitution of the United States is hereby repealed.

Section 2

The transportation or importation into any state, territory, or possession of the United States for delivery or use therein of intoxicating liquors, in violation of the laws thereof, is hereby prohibited.

Section 3

This article shall be inoperative unless it shall have been ratified as an amendment to the Constitution by conventions in the several states, as provided in the Constitution, within seven years from the date of the submission hereof to the states by the Congress.

Chapter 3: Frank's Start as an Artist

Frank first began singing in his parents' bar, where he spent his afternoons as a child. Patrons put nickels into a player piano, and Frank was expected to sing along with the purchased tune. When Frank was fifteen, in 1931, his mother's brother Dominick bought Frank a ukulele. At the time, ukuleles were in fashion, and Frank showed off his ability to play on the street corner, at a high school halftime show, and at his mother's parties. Music was becoming a bigger and bigger part of Frank's life. One night, after going to see Bing Crosby in concert with Nancy, Frank declared his ambition to become a famous singer.

Frank's career choice of high school dropout and aspiring musician did not sit well with his parents, especially as the country entered the Great Depression and people despaired for work. While Dolly was more supportive of Frank's interest in music than Marty, who wouldn't allow Frank to practice singing inside of the house except in the basement, she too lost patience with Frank's inability to hold what she considered a real job. When Frank was seventeen, the tension peaked, and Marty told Frank to leave the house. Marty and Frank didn't speak for about a year.

Renting a room in New York City, Frank scrambled to make enough money to eat and pay rent but found himself immersed in a rich musical scene. Jazz music was exploding in the same clubs where Frank was singing for little or no pay, and Frank saw musicians who would later become legendary, including Billie Holiday, Benny Goodman, and Tommy Dorsey. He admired the music of the largely black jazz community of musicians and was an early supporter of racial equality.

After some time, Frank's parents seemed to relent from their earlier hardheartedness toward Frank's lofty ambitions. Dolly bought him a sound system that included a microphone, which was an expensive purchase at the time. Frank by this time had realized that his instrument was the microphone. With its technology, he could reach audiences with his voice in an intimate way.

Around Frank's eighteenth birthday, he reconciled with his parents and moved home. He began to get more opportunities to perform and even won a contest at the State Theater in Jersey City. He also got onto the radio occasionally. Dolly used her political and social connections to make Frank the fourth member of a three-man band who called themselves the Three Flashes, whom she knew because they were customers of her saloon. They agreed to allow Frank to audition with them for a radio-show competition. Calling themselves the Hoboken Four, the group won the contest and a six-month contract touring around the country.

Now almost twenty years old, Frank took advantage of the trip's opportunities to seduce many women. His voice made him attractive to women, and it became clear that he had special talent. However, the tour was grueling, and the band members fought, sometimes physically, leading Frank to quit after about three months.

Back home, he again scraped for singing gigs on the local radio, at cultural clubs, and anyplace that would have him. In 1937 he reached out to his relative Ray Sinatra, a musician working for the NBC house orchestra. Ray helped Frank get an appearance on an NBC radio show. No further opportunities came from the appearance. Frank considered quitting singing but continued to grab onto whatever practice and exposure he could get.

During his gigs in Manhattan, Frank met an industry recruiter named Hank Sanicola, who befriended Frank. Hank helped Frank by literally using his strong build to get him into clubs, and he assisted Frank financially by slipping him money every week. Frank's friends in the music business instructed Frank to take lessons from the burgeoning opera scene, advice that Frank took to heart. Frank also took voice lessons on the advice of Hank, studying at home for hours a day. He polished up his grammar as well and advertised himself as a vocalist and recording artist. Still, by age twenty-two, his music career floundering, Frank was considering giving up music when he got a pivotal gig at the Rustic Cabin.

Bing Crosby in Brief

Bing Crosby was born on May 3, 1903. His parents named him Harry Lillis, and he became "Bing" at age seven because of his adoration of a comic strip called "The Bingville Bugle."

Bing went to LA to seek his fortune in the mid 1920s. He performed in vaudeville and later joined a jazz band. In 1931 Bing's radio program made him a nearly instant success. The show was on the air for almost thirty years.

Admired for his charm—and, perhaps, in spite of his looks—Bing signed on with Paramount and became a star of the silver screen in the 1930s. This, coupled with his radio show, gave him the fame he had been hoping for. The *Road To* films, in which he appeared with Bob Hope and Dorothy Lamour, are part of his lasting legacy. Bing and Bob developed a bond that extended past their on-screen rapport, and they became lifelong friends.

Bing was married twice and had seven children. After his death in 1977, some of his children claimed that Bing was an abusive father while others disputed this claim. Fans of his many movies and number-one hit songs remember Bing for his talent and laid-back on-screen persona.

The Great Depression in Brief

From 1929 through 1939, the United States of America suffered economic troubles known as the Great Depression. The stock market crashed in October of 1929, and consumer spending and investment declined steadily for years afterward. At its worst, the Great Depression saw more than 20 percent of America's population, at least twelve million people, unemployed and almost half of America's banks failing.

In 1932 Franklin Delano Roosevelt was elected president. His New Deal programs, which included ways to improve the industrial and agriculture sectors as well as financial-system reforms, are generally credited with easing some of the burden of the Great Depression.

World War II began in Europe in 1939. America agreed to support Britain and France, and wartime production helped pull the country out of the Great Depression. When America declared war in 1941 after the Pearl Harbor attack, production and conscription eased the unemployment rate.

Chapter 4: Frank Sinatra, Rustic Cabin Boy and Lover

Frank wanted to work at a nightclub called the Rustic Cabin, a job that, though it didn't pay very well, would give him the opportunity to gain exposure on the radio and, thereby, to the talent scouts who monitored the radio. After hearing Frank crying in his room after being rejected from yet another singing job, Dolly swung into action with characteristic vigor. Dolly claimed that she used political connections to help Frank obtain work at the Rustic Cabin. Likely, Dolly's friends were really more powerful than that—Dolly knew people in the Mafia (see chapter 9). No matter how exactly it happened, Frank got the job at the Rustic Cabin.

As much as Frank had wanted the job, he found it unglamorous and frustrating. Most of the job involved waiting tables and emceeing. However, it gave Frank the chance to sing—and to meet women. At the Rustic Cabin, Frank sang in front of famous musicians such as Cole Porter and Tommy Dorsey, although he demonstrated some of the stage fright that affected him most of his career, forgetting the words when told of his important audience members.

The most immediate result of his performances was the opportunity to meet and seduce women, an opportunity of which he took advantage despite his seven-year relationship with Nancy Barbato. While Frank wasn't traditionally handsome—he was very skinny, and many noted that his ears stuck out from his head—his voice and the intimate way in which he sang made him very attractive to women. Several lovers from that time later described him as a "cuddler" who wasn't much in bed but was very endearing; and some women later remarked on how large his genitalia were in comparison to his skinny frame.

Frank's dalliances were not all innocuous in nature. At the Rustic Cabin, Frank met Toni Della Penta, a temperamental Italian American woman, whom Frank dated for several months and eventually promised to marry. Upon becoming "engaged" to Frank, Toni slept with him and claimed to become pregnant. She fought with Nancy at the Cabin and had Frank arrested twice, once for "seduction" and once for "adultery," both criminal charges at the time.

Dolly sent her husband to talk to Toni's father, and eventually Toni, who was technically married to another man, backed off—but not before the press had published stories about both arrests. In response, Frank demonstrated what was to become his famously violent temper, telling a newspaper worker that he would kill anyone who had anything do with the articles.

Shortly after the Toni Della Penta affair, Frank and Nancy married. They wed on February 4, 1939, in a small ceremony at a church in Jersey City. They had been dating for seven years, since Nancy was fourteen years old. While Nancy thought her husband appeared to be happier than he had ever been, other friends of both the bride and groom experienced foreboding for the couple. Frank's own close friends and music promoters, Nick Sevano and Hank Sanicola, expressed pity for Nancy, whom they remembered as very nervous about Frank's relationships with other women. One friend stated that Frank told Nancy early on that he was "going to the top" and wasn't about to be dragged down by her or anyone else.

Regardless, Frank and Nancy moved into an apartment in Jersey City. During the first years of their marriage, money was tight since Frank made little at the Rustic Cabin. Nancy worked as a secretary despite Frank's belief that a wife should not have to work outside the home.

Frank was getting desperate at the Rustic Cabin and started taking whatever singing gigs he could get, with or without pay, just to get exposure. He fumbled his first chances at impressing people who could help him move up in the world, forgetting the words to the song he was singing at Rustic Cabin when told that Cole Porter was in the audience and becoming flustered when Tommy Dorsey walked in while he was rehearsing at another club.

The famous Glen Miller and Tommy Dorsey were not impressed when they heard Frank sing for the first time. Finally, though, Frank got a break when Harry James, a talented trumpet-player who was in the process of forming his own band, came to the Rustic Cabin to hear Frank sing on the advice of Harry's wife, who had heard Frank on the radio. Harry hired Frank on the spot, and Frank took Nancy with him on his tour with Harry James's band.

Chapter 5: Frank Sinatra Makes the Big Time

Harry James, a talented twenty-three-year-old musician, focused on Frank's biggest strength—his ability to imbue the lyrics with feeling. He tried to convince Frank to change his last name to Satin, but Frank, sensitive to the prejudice he faced because of his Italian heritage, proudly refused. Frank began recording with Harry, and while none of the records immediately became hits, his song "All or Nothing at All" would later soar in the charts upon being rereleased.

Overall, the tour did not go well, and Frank and Nancy found themselves sharing shabby quarters with other band members and struggling for money. When Nancy became pregnant, she returned home to New Jersey. Tommy Dorsey offered Frank a chance to audition, and Frank leaped at it. Tommy remembered him as "the kid who blew the lyrics" earlier but was impressed with what he heard on this audition. He offered Frank a position, and, despite being in a contract with Harry James, Frank took it immediately. Harry graciously allowed Frank to break the contract, and Frank played with the James band for the last time in early 1940. When the band bus pulled out after that performance without Frank, Frank began to cry. He regarded Harry as a friend and mentor and stayed on good terms with him for the rest of his life.

In January 1940, Frank took a huge step up in joining Tommy Dorsey's band. Tommy was a perfectionist with a famously cantankerous personality. He was also a very talented musician who demanded that his band members adhere to rigorously high standards of practice and appearance. Like Frank, Tommy was an insomniac, a heavy drinker, and a womanizer.

Frank won Tommy's affection by inviting him to eat with Frank and a friend after noticing that Tommy always ate alone after their shows. Tommy, in return, listened to Frank's requests on behalf of the band members and taught him his secrets of breath control. Frank shared Tommy's high standards and practiced for hours on end with his old singing coach and Hank Sanicola. Around this time, Frank saw a concert at Carnegie Hall and became entranced with classical music.

In May 1940, Frank experienced an important night. The Dorsey band was playing at the Astor Hotel, and several celebrities were in attendance. When Frank sang his solo songs, the audience erupted with applause and begged for more. Since the band had no more solo songs prepared for Frank, Frank winged it with a performance of "Smoke Gets in Your Eyes." The crowd loved Frank, and all summer long, the club was packed with people eager to hear him.

With Tommy, Frank also saw his first recorded hits. Tommy and Frank capitalized on the public's love of hearing about loneliness, turning out "I'll Never Smile Again," "Everything Happens to Me," and "I Guess I'll Have to Dream the Rest." While Frank didn't make a lot of money from these hits, his name was becoming recognized, and his voice known.

Frank continued to take advantage of his opportunities to sleep with women. Nancy, who had become pregnant during the James tour, found out about Frank's affair with an actress in Las Vegas shortly after her daughter was born. Frank apologized and swore he would do better. However, the marriage continued to crumble as Frank traveled far and wide and met many alluring women. Frank later admitted that he should never have married Nancy and that he mistook the warmth and friendship he had found with her and her family as a lonely teenage boy for love. Nancy, a traditional Italian American woman, wanted a husband who was serious about family and home, but by the time they married, Frank had already decided to escape his old neighborhood and the family he had made there.

Meanwhile, Frank began to outpoll Bing Crosby, the number one singer in the nation, among college students. Frank's mounting fame caused some problems for his position with the Dorsey band. Frank's ego was growing, and his temper becoming worse than ever before. He spoke down to a female co-singer, making it clear that he thought she was "backwards" because of her Southern roots. He especially fought with the talented drummer Buddy Rich, who resented Frank's stealing of the show. The two fought physically, and at one point Frank allegedly hired two men to beat Buddy up.

Tommy, who demanded that his band members follow strict rules, became frustrated with Frank. Frank was similarly frustrated at having to follow all of Tommy's rules, and in the fall of 1941, he gave Tommy a year's notice of his leaving the band. Tommy, infuriated, refused to release Frank from his contract but did raise Frank's pay and allow him to record as a soloist. Frank's recorded songs, which included "Night and Day," "The Night We Called It a Day," The Song Is You," and "Lamplight Serenade," were all hits, and Frank climbed in rank next to Bing Crosby as one of the most popular singers in the country.

Still, Frank chafed under his contract with Tommy. He tried to get Tommy to fire him by showing up late to rehearsals and breaking other rules, but Tommy told him that he would hold Frank to the next two years of his contract. Finally, in the fall of 1942, Tommy agreed to let Frank break the contract but not without making Frank sign a release document, by which Frank agreed to severe penalties. The penalties included Tommy's right to a significant chunk of Frank's future profits.

The following year, as Frank continued to make big money, Tommy sued to enforce the contract. Frank hired an attorney named Henry Jaffe, well known in the entertainment industry, to negotiate a deal. According to Frank, Jaffe used his connections with the radio industry to strong-arm Tommy into making a deal, threatening to block Tommy's ability to broadcast on NBC if Tommy did not agree. A decade later, Tommy revealed that he was threatened by the Mafia to back off (see chapter 9). Whatever the true story, Tommy released Frank from the penalties for breaking his contract.

Tommy Dorsey in Brief

Born on November 19, 1905, Tommy Dorsey was a trumpet and trombone player, although he was most famous for his trombone playing. He and his brother Jimmy (musical talent ran in the family) were the two main components of the Dorsey Brothers Orchestra.

In the mid 1930s, the brothers had a falling out, and Tommy Dorsey formed the Tommy Dorsey Orchestra without Jimmy. In the 1950s, the brothers played together again when Jimmy joined the Tommy Dorsey Orchestra, apparently reconciling after their old fight. Tommy Dorsey died soon after, on November 26, 1956.

Tommy's trombone playing was a major part of the swing-music scene that was prevalent in the 1930s and 1940s. His nickname was the "sentimental gentleman of swing." Tommy was married three times, with two children from his first marriage. Doctors attributed his premature death to eating a big meal and then choking in his sleep.

Buddy Rich in Brief

The two words you are most likely to have heard in conjunction with Buddy Rich are "drummer" and "legendary." Born on September 30, 1917, Buddy Rich was exposed to the entertainment world when he performed in vaudeville as a child. As a drummer, and as a singer and dancer, Buddy was a child star.

Unlike with so many of today's child stars, Buddy's marketability did not peter out, and he drummed with many swing bands, big bands, and jazz bands, including the orchestras of Harry James, Tommy Dorsey, and Artie Shaw. Buddy's first band of his own was funded by Frank Sinatra. That early orchestra failed, but a later one was successful and played together for many years. Self-taught and lightning fast, Buddy drummed nearly up until his death in 1987.

His temper was as quick as his drumming. He and Frank had many fights, and Buddy notoriously ranted at his band members when they didn't meet his expectations. Buddy suffered multiple heart attacks; but, in the end, a brain tumor caused his death on April 2, 1987.

Chapter 6: The Attack of the Bobbysoxers

Frank's plan to sign a high-paying contract with Columbia Records after leaving the Dorsey band was foiled when labor disputes effectively shut down the recording studio for two years. After casting around a bit on the West Coast, trying and failing to get positions with TV networks, Frank came back to New York. There he had the luck of getting the attention of Robert Weitman, the director of the Paramount Theater, Broadway's biggest music venue. After seeing the small but intense crowd of New Jersey teenagers Frank attracted to his audience, Weitman added Frank to the Paramount's New Year's Eve lineup, side by side with huge names like Benny Goodman and Bing Crosby. While Frank was fairly unknown nationally, the New York audience went insane when he took the stage. Frank was a hit. His booking at the Paramount Theater was extended to two months.

Frank's fans at the Paramount primarily included young teenage girls, known as "bobbysoxers" because of the traditional school uniform of the day, which consisted of white socks and knee-length skirts. The girls' screams shook the theater, a never-before-heard phenomenon, suggesting the consumer power of the young-teenage-female demographic. Girls skipped school and spent all day in the theater, urinating on the seats rather than getting up to use the restroom. Underwear and brassieres were thrown onto the stage.

As good as the publicity was, these fans put Frank's reputation with an older, wealthier audience at risk. When the Paramount gig ended and Frank began performing at Riobamba nightclub, the club owner worried that Frank would not succeed outside of pleasing "the kids" who were his fans. Frank shared his concern.

They had nothing to worry about. Frank blew the other performers at the club out of the water and soon became the headliner. He was reported to have a magical control over the audience, who became hushed in awe when Frank began to sing.

After another month at the Paramount, Frank did something rare for a pop musician: he performed with the symphony orchestras of several major U.S. cities. Next he was off to Hollywood, starring in the movies *Higher and Higher* and *Anchors Aweigh*. For *Anchors Aweigh*, Frank worked hard under Gene Kelly's tutelage to learn how to dance.

When Frank returned to the Paramount for opening night in 1944, a mob of teenage girls swarmed Times Square. Similar mobs waited for Frank in Chicago, Boston, and Pittsburgh. America had never seen this type of mass hysteria for an entertainer, which, indeed, was only matched during that century by the public's reactions to Elvis Presley and the Beatles.

Frank's effect on young girls was likely part-real and part-staged by his publicity managers. While Frank's voice undoubtedly had a strong impact on a number of young women, causing some truly to "swoon," or faint, others did so for mere effect or because they were paid to do so by Frank's booking agent and his assistants.

Frank was now making serious money and had a paid security detail as well as a team of musical experts as his composers, arrangers, and general assistants. Frank openly threatened any would-be hecklers with his team of muscle, though he was also known to be generous to a fault. He began dressing in dark, stylish suits and was reputed to have a huge wardrobe.

Now the opposite of poor, Frank moved Nancy into a house in Hasbruck Heights, New Jersey; but this was only for a brief time before relocating the family permanently to the Los Angeles area, where Frank had signed a movie contract with MGM. It was late in 1944, and Nancy had just given birth to a son, Franklin Wayne Emmanuel Sinatra.

The new family house was luxurious and situated on the beautiful shores of Toluca Lake. Frank filled the house with famous friends and hosted parties on his raft, parked off of his dock. Nancy and Frank put up a front of marital harmony and domestic happiness; but behind the scenes, they drifted further and further apart. Many of Nancy's family members moved from New Jersey to be near her, and Frank grew irritated at the constant flow of family visitors.

As hard as Nancy tried to fill the glamorous shoes of the wife of the famous Frank Sinatra, she wanted a traditional family full of relatives and old-fashioned loyalty. Frank, in the meantime, kept a list in his Hollywood dressing room of women with whom he wanted to have sex—and crossed off many names as he succeeded in his conquests.

Gene Kelly in Brief

As a dancer, singer, and movie star, Gene Kelly embodied the golden era of musicals in Hollywood. Born on August 2, 1912, Gene came to dancing with the outlook and physique of an athlete. He was known for his masculine style of dancing.

Gene Kelly's best-known role was his lead in *Singin' in the Rain*. Before that 1952 hit, he starred in multiple movies with Frank Sinatra, including *Anchors Aweigh* and *On the Town*. The masculine, athletic dancer made a good pairing with Frank Sinatra; it's difficult to imagine Frank starring alongside some of the more romantic top-hat-and-tails waltzers of the time.

In the 1960s and 1970s, Gene worked more in television than on the big screen. In the 1980s and 1990s, he mostly stayed away from the spotlight. He died on February 2, 1996.

Chapter 7: Frank Sinatra, Draft Dodger

On December 7, 1941, the Japanese attacked Pearl Harbor, bringing the United States into World War II. Frank was living in Hollywood. He was attending a party at Lana Turner's house the day that the attack occurred. The United States' entrance into the war changed Frank's professional life in two major ways: first, he became a suspected draft-dodger; and, second, the music scene changed drastically after the war.

With America's entrance into the war, many celebrities made news by joining the armed forces, including Clark Gable, Jimmy Stewart, and Joe DiMaggio. In late 1940, a draft was instituted. Frank reported as required but was found ineligible for service because he was a married father.

In 1943 Frank was reclassified as eligible for service but was declared ineligible under the "4-F" classification, which disqualified men "for physical, mental or moral reasons." A punctured eardrum sustained either during his traumatic forceps birth or in one of Frank's many brawls was the most commonly cited reason for this classification.

Some of his fans found this explanation unsatisfactory, and a rumor that Frank was purposefully dodging the draft began to circulate. At a show at the Paramount in 1944, someone threw an egg at Frank, hitting him in the eye. His picture outside the theater was soiled with tomatoes that had been thrown by angry sailors.

The army summoned Frank twice more for physical exams to evaluate his eligibility for service, and twice more Frank was found unfit for service. The public scoffed at one of the classifications used, 2-A(F), which was used for persons who were found qualified for military service but were deferred for "national health, safety, or interest."

Publicly, Frank proclaimed that he very much wanted to serve, but the mystery surrounding his lack of fitness to serve was never fully cleared up. Most biographers suspect that he could have served if he had wanted to. Other information that emerged after Sinatra's death implies that Frank might have been found unfit because he revealed to the army doctors that he suffered from anxiety and mental instability.

Frank joined the war effort in other ways: he sang at several rallies, performed at concerts for military groups, and appeared on a radio program made for servicemen abroad. He organized clothing drives and auctioned off his own clothes to raise money for the war. He did not, however, perform for troops in the line of danger even as many other celebrities sang on this "Foxhole Circuit."

Biographers speculate that Frank may have been less intimidated by the actual danger posed by performing in unsecured areas of Europe than by the American soldiers' potentially scathing reception of him as a perceived draft dodger. When Frank did tour the European USO circuit in May 1945, he portrayed himself as a skinny, average Joe, endearing himself to the troops, whom he thanked profusely. The troops had "The Voice," Sinatra's nickname, painted on the fronts of planes and vehicles.

Frank faced another challenge as a result of the changing cultural and musical scene in the United States after the war. His former fans, the teenage girls in bobbysocks, were now marrying the flood of returning soldiers and abandoning their childhood idols. The baby boom began, and families moved out of cities to the suburbs.

Swing music was dying out and being replaced by bebop and a looser style of jazz. New styles of music were embraced as the country put the war in its past, and Frank wasn't sure where he would fit in. In response, Frank devoted himself to his film career and, surprisingly for a celebrity of that time, to politics.

Lana Turner in Brief

Beautiful enough to be discovered while casually drinking a soda, Lana Turner became the ultimate sex symbol in the glamorous days of the silver screen. Born on February 8, 1921, Lana and her mother moved frequently after her father, a bootlegger, was murdered.

Lana first appeared in movies at the age of fifteen after her legendary discovery by a Hollywood agent. In addition to appearing in many movies, Lana was known as "the sweater girl." Posters of her in form-fitting sweaters were commonplace amongst lonely soldiers abroad. Later in her career, Lana worked hard to reshape her image. She did so successfully and acted in numerous roles that showcased her talents beyond wearing a sweater well.

Lana had a long career, acting until her retirement in 1982. She was married seven times and had affairs with many stars, including Frank Sinatra. She died on June 29, 1997.

Chapter 8: Frank Sinatra, Political Activist and Suspected Communist

From a young age, Frank had been immersed in politics due to his mother's civic career. He was a staunch Democrat and was among the first celebrities to use his fame to promote political causes. His politics were based not only on his upbringing but also on a great deal of reading: Frank had begun reading in-depth books about politics and American literature while touring with the Dorsey band.

When Franklin Roosevelt ran for re-election in 1944 against Republican candidate Thomas Dewey, Frank became actively involved. Working with the Democratic Party, he appeared at fundraisers, spoke at Carnegie Hall, and appeared on broadcasts in support of Roosevelt. Frank was invited to, and attended, an afternoon reception at the White House during this time even though it earned FDR some negative press for wasting time with a "crooner." He appeared with FDR's running mate, Harry Truman, at a huge event in Madison Square Garden the week before the election and attended two to three campaign events a day immediately prior to the election. Frank spent election night drinking with Orson Welles at a New York restaurant. Allegedly, Frank, in his drunken state, made public threats to beat up a journalist who had written in opposition of Roosevelt, and he went so far as to damage the journalist's hotel room. Frank was devastated when FDR died soon after the election.

Frank spoke of his own hypothetical political ambitions, revealing that he thought holding office was a service to the community. He viewed his political activity as his duty as a citizen. Frank's political activity had other ramifications as well. When the anti-communist fervor hit the United States, it hit Hollywood particularly hard. Frank Sinatra was a tough-talking, politically active, wealthy singer and actor who was proud of his immigrant, working-class roots. This made him a prime suspect of being a communist spy, in the view of the United States government.

In the 1930s, communism had existed as a relatively acceptable political party in the U.S., with American Communists backing President Roosevelt. By the end of the Second World War, the United States had begun its long conflict with the Soviet regime, and right-wing politicians began their witch-hunt for communist infiltrators of the United States government.

Frank, famous and cocky, continued his loud support of "the little guy," a philosophy that he had championed in his support of Roosevelt's campaign. Frank contributed to a number of causes that the House Un-American Activities Committee (HUAC) considered suspect, including the Committee for Yugoslav Relief, the World Youth Conference, the Independent Citizens Committee of the Arts, Sciences, and Professions (ICCASP), and its Hollywood branch, the

HICCASP. Frank was elected vice-chairman of the most suspect of these, the ICCASP. The FBI began intercepting Frank's letters and investigated his suspected involvement in a large espionage case involving Frank's dentist, Dr. Abraham Weinstein.

The FBI and HUAC never found any solid evidence linking Frank Sinatra to espionage or to the Communist party. Still, after the Committee was twice called to investigate Frank Sinatra, his publicists became more sensitive about the accusations and went out of their way to portray Frank as anti-communist. Frank reacted with his characteristic temper, scoffing that anyone who supported "the little guy" or veterans' rights would be labeled a communist. He joined a group of other celebrities in forming the Committee for the First Amendment, which protested HUAC's witch-hunting ways. Even so, he approached the FBI to try to clear his name and offer any information that might be helpful, an offer that was refused. He was prohibited from performing for U.S. troops after the Korean War. Frank fumed over these injustices.

FDR in Brief

Franklin Delano Roosevelt, who was assistant secretary of the navy under President Wilson and the thirty-second president of the United States, was born in New York in 1882. He had early ambitions to follow his distant cousin, President Theodore Roosevelt, into politics. Early in his career, he was elected to the New York senate. In addition to his appointment under Wilson, he was the Democratic vice-presidential candidate following Wilson's last term.

When he was thirty-nine, he contracted the poliovirus and lost the use of his legs. He worked hard to regain his mobility and eventually moved around on crutches.

His illness did not stop him, and he was elected president of the United States in 1932. He served four terms as president. He was president during the Great Depression and World War II, famously telling Americans, "The only thing we have to fear is fear itself." Roosevelt's New Deal programs were designed to bring America back from the Depression.

President Roosevelt died in 1945, near the end of World War II.

Chapter 9: Frank Sinatra, Mob Collaborator

Despite the common misconception that equates the Mob with the Sicilian *La Cosa Nostra* and blames the emergence of the American Mob on the rush of Italian immigrants, the Mob was actually created by the perceived injustices of Prohibition. The Mob originally was an alliance of Jews, Italians, and Irishmen who orchestrated the production and distribution of alcohol during the nearly fourteen years that Prohibition remained the law of the land. Perceived as an anti-immigrant law, Prohibition united Italian crime bosses from Sicily, which did have a history of organized crime, and bosses from the north of Italy, along with other immigrant and first-generation gangsters.

Frank, growing up in his parents' illegal bar, was immersed in the culture of the Mafia from a young age. The man who became the head of the American Mafia, Luciano, came from the same tiny Sicilian town as Marty Sinatra's parents. Dolly's two brothers, Dominick and Lawrence, were both heavily involved in criminal activity and were linked to famous mobsters. Lawrence lived with the Sinatras for a time after getting out of jail, and Frank was very close to him. Much evidence exists that Frank was intimately involved with the Mafia, especially with Lucky Luciano and Willie Moretti, a New Jersey crime boss.

Both during and after Prohibition, the Mafia controlled major segments of the entertainment industry. One avenue of control was the Mafia's strategic investment in artists and performers. Mob bosses controlled which records were played on jukeboxes, and thus which songs became hits, to make sure their investments paid off.

At age twenty-two, his music career floundering, Frank was considering giving up music when he got a pivotal gig at the Rustic Cabin. Despite Dolly's story that she used political connections to get Frank the job, plenty of evidence points to the real connection being Dolly's friendship with a minor mobster named Gyp De Carlo. De Carlo was a close associate of Luciano's who managed the Mob's interest in singers. Dolly knew De Carlo from local politics and family connections; and Frank got the Rustic Cabin job.

While Frank remained evasive all his life about his participation in the Mafia, telling the press that he only knew famous mobsters because they happened to frequent the same saloons and nightclubs that he did, Frank later admitted that Moretti had made some bookings for him to perform early in his career. Luciano, by then controlling the Mafia from his jail cell, was told good things about Frank's talent by his associates Costello and Moretti. Law enforcement reports record that Moretti at some point admitted he had a financial interest in Frank Sinatra. An informant named Chico Scimone confirmed that Moretti arranged an audition for Frank Sinatra for the chief Mob bosses. Frank had begun a long relationship with the Mob, one that would serve him, and endanger him, for the rest of his career.

Frank's involvement with the Mafia did not stop at the Rustic Cabin. After later signing a contract with the Tommy Dorsey band, with which he became famous, Frank may have used his Mob allies to get him out of the hefty penalty that he faced for breaking his contract with Tommy. According to Tommy, Willie Moretti and two other mobsters paid him a visit, letting Tommy know the lethal consequences of failing to back down. Tommy reported that he took the hint and settled the contract with Frank. Frank's release from the contract terms made him known in the federal law enforcement world as a Mob collaborator.

In early 1947, Frank made a misstep that publicized his involvement with the Mafia to the world. On a trip to Miami, Frank stayed in the home of famous mobster Joe Fischetti along with several other well-known members of the Mob. The trip took place shortly after crime boss Luciano had been released from prison on the condition that he return to Italy and stay out of the United States. Luciano, still very much in control of the Mob, did go back to Italy for a brief time but quickly moved into new headquarters in Havana, Cuba, from where he could be in close contact with American mobsters. A well-known picture shows Joe and Rocco Fischetti disembarking from a plane in Havana, accompanied by none other than Frank Sinatra. Frank was seen repeatedly over the next four days with Luciano and other mobsters, and the American press soon publicized that fact.

Frank immediately denied any association with the Mob, claiming that he had accidentally "run into" the Fischettis in Miami, that he had coincidentally taken the same plane as the mobsters to Cuba, and that he merely accepted a dinner invitation to an event that included Lucky Luciano, unbeknownst to Frank until he got to the table. Frank also vacillated on his story about who had introduced him to Luciano. Moreover, Frank claimed that he hadn't known of Luciano's reputation as a Mob crime boss, an implausible claim given Luciano's international fame and the fact that the two men's families came from the same small town in Sicily.

The FBI, whose file on Frank is nearly a thousand pages long between his suspected communist activities and his Mafia involvement, has evidence indicating that Frank had met with the Fischettis on an ongoing basis for the three months before the Havana trip. Staff at the Hotel Nacional in Havana, where Luciano, the Fischettis, and Frank stayed, reported the men's activities to the press. Frank may have carried money for the Mob during the Havana trip, and still more reports state that Frank carried money for the Mob on other occasions, nearly getting caught once in New York City with a briefcase filled with two million dollars of Mob money.

Frank denied all of these claims and even sued newspapers for libel over the stories about his time in Havana. Frank absolutely denied having any business with the Mob or any interaction with mobsters other than a passing handshake, a fact that was repeatedly contradicted by FBI informants who overheard mobsters stating that they had a financial interest in Frank Sinatra.

After the publicity inspired by the Havana episode, fanned by Frank's presence, the FBI was successful in getting Cuba to send Luciano back to Italy. But evidence shows that Frank and Luciano stayed in touch and that Frank met up with Luciano in Italy and during Luciano's surreptitious trips to the United States. FBI informants claimed that Frank transported money to Luciano on at least two more occasions. A newspaper published an article saying that Italian police had found a silver lighter from Frank Sinatra in

Luciano's apartment with the inscription "To my dear friend Luciano."

A lover of Frank's from that time period confirms that Frank indeed consorted with individuals whom he had to keep secret. In his later life, Frank grew wiser about his contact with Luciano. He limited his contact to telephone calls and mail. Many sources confirm that Frank and Luciano were dear friends, with Frank admiring and "hero-worshipping" Luciano, who in turn bore a great deal of respect and affection for Frank. Frank also could not deny close friendships with other mobsters, including Jilly Rizzo (see chapter 20) and Al Pacella (see chapter 22).

Frank's friends in the Mafia would come through for him again, providing him work when he fell from the spotlight and getting him a key role in the movie *From Here to Eternity* (see chapter 14). Frank also co-ran a casino in Las Vegas, the Sands, with Mafia money (see chapter 18).

Frank also ran the risks that accompanied doing business with the Mob, nearly losing his life when he served as an intermediary between the Kennedy family and the Mafia (see chapter 18) and when he withdrew from supporting a Mafia-run organization, the Italian American Civil Rights League (see chapter 20). Frank was also subpoenaed to testify before the Kefauver Committee, a special Senate committee dedicated to investigating organized crime, as well as in several other criminal investigations (see chapters 20 and 22).

Lucky Luciano in Brief

Born in Sicily with the name Salvatore Luciana, on November 24, 1897, Charles "Lucky" Luciano came to the United States with his family in the early part of the century. He dropped out of high school and ended up in a reformatory in 1916 for selling heroin. He had been associating with and doing jobs for mobsters for years by this time.

The Prohibition era served Luciano well. He made his name and fortune bootlegging in the 1920s. In 1931 Luciano helped assassinate a Mob boss, whose position he took as a head of one of the Five Families in New York. After he assassinated another rival, he became the boss of bosses and focused on making crime truly "organized" and profitable with his National Crime Syndicate.

In 1936 he received a sentence of thirty to fifty years for running brothels. Luciano spent his time in prison aiding the war effort and was paroled and deported after the war. He went first to Italy, then to Cuba. Cuba soon sent him to Naples, where he remained until he died in January 1962.

Chapter 10: Frank Sinatra, Civil Rights Leader

Although fabulously rich, Frank never forgot that he came from a poor area of New Jersey—or the prejudice that he experienced there as an Italian at a time when Italians were not considered equal to other European Americans. He was an early supporter of racial and religious equality before such support was mainstream. He contributed to the NAACP, stating that it wasn't just black people who were hanged, referring to the mob that lynched the Italians who were not convicted of killing a New Orleans politician.

In his daily life, he smarted at the racism he saw exercised against his African-American colleagues. In the 1940s and 1950s, black Americans were not permitted to stay at the same hotels as whites and were segregated in many important ways. Frank went out of his way to find African American musicians when he recorded, at a time when orchestras were normally segregated. He befriended, and fostered the career of, African American performer Sammy Davis Jr., and he refused to enter the establishments that wouldn't let Sammy in. Later, Frank was the best man in Sammy Davis' controversial wedding to a white woman.

Frank also used his fame to further the cause of racial and religious equality. He made many speaking appearances, addressing audiences on the topic of racial tolerance. He was especially interested in influencing America's youth on the issue and spoke at high schools where there had been racial violence. He raised large sums of money for Martin Luther King Jr.'s causes and made a movie about interracial marriage. Frank wrote an article about prejudice for the black magazine *Ebony*, denouncing the immorality of racism. The fact that a public white figure would even write for a black magazine caused a stir at the time.

Frank was also a vocal champion of religious equality, especially supporting Jewish causes in the wake of the Holocaust. He won an Academy Award for the short film *The House I Live In*, in which Frank, as himself, breaks up a gang of boys who are beating up a young Jewish boy and teaches them about racial and religious tolerance. He wore a mezuzah that his Jewish neighbor had given him as a child, and he supported the Zionist cause. On one occasion, he served as a carrier of a large amount of money for one of the main military branches of the pro-Israel underground movement, facilitating the shipment of arms from New York City to Israel in violation of an American embargo on sending arms to the Middle East.

Frank recognized later that the creation of the Israeli state had disadvantages for the Arab population, and he tried to work toward causes that helped both Arabs and Jews. He created a youth center in Nazareth for both Arab and Jewish children. Despite his attempt to work for Arabs' human rights, the Arab League countries banned his records and movies for years, and Osama Bin Laden was said to hate him. Saddam Hussein, however, was allegedly a fan of Sinatra's and enjoyed dancing to his music.

Frank's outrage about racial inequality was also demonstrated in less appropriate ways. As a kid on the streets of Hoboken, he had internalized that the correct response when someone called him a "dirty Guinea" or another racial slur was to beat the pulp out of the offender. He continued this practice as an adult, punching out a journalist who called a fellow partygoer an anti-Semitic slur and hitting a waiter who refused to serve lunch to a black companion.

He often sang "Ole Man River," which is traditionally sung by a black man and mentions that the white folks play while the "darkies" work. Frank changed the lyrics to reflect that the white men played while "we" worked, including himself in the category of the oppressed.

One night while drinking in Tel Aviv during a movie shoot, Frank drunkenly insisted on trying to call a Nazi collaborator, shouting the collaborator's name at the operator and demolishing the hotel phone. Whenever he wanted an excuse for roughing up a journalist or other person, Frank claimed that the victim had made a racial slur about him—a claim that was rarely true. Frank also liked to challenge racism and stereotypes by making racist jokes, with the idea that such humor ridiculed true prejudice. Most of his jokes were playful in nature, but some were truly offensive.

Sammy Davis Jr. in Brief

Sammy Davis Jr., born December 8, 1925, started his career when quite young, in vaudeville. He kept performing until he joined the army during World War II. He experienced severe racism in the armed services, and fellow soldiers even physically attacked him.

After the war, Sammy Davis Jr. sang and performed stand-up. He was popular enough that when he refused to perform in segregated clubs, some clubs integrated.

In 1954 Sammy Davis Jr. lost his eye as the result of a car accident. While in the hospital, he began exploring Judaism, and he converted from Christianity soon after. The singer and performer became well known for his roles in movies and as a member of the Rat Pack. He was married three times and had three children. Sammy Davis Jr. died on May 16, 1990.

Chapter 11: Frank and Lana

Frank once joked with a group of writers that if he had slept with as many women as he was rumored to have, he wouldn't be alive. However, there is no doubt that Frank had a hectic extramarital sex life. His publicist, George Evans, helped him keep up the front of a good family man; Frank even published articles about the moral wholesomeness of marriage. The reality, however, was a very different picture.

Many nights, Nancy stayed at the family estate in Toluca Lake with her and Frank's two children while Frank went to an apartment in Wilshire Towers rented by band-mates. At the apartment, the men entertained call girls and girlfriends. Under friends' names, Frank is rumored to have rented his own apartment as well, which he used to entertain his sex guests. Frank's FBI records reflect reports that Frank frequently purchased the services of prostitutes.

Newspapers published daily gossip columns about which Hollywood beauty was seen out with Frank the previous night. Among the actresses with whom Frank had long-term, on-and-off affairs were Shirley Ballard, Marilyn Maxwell, and Marlene Dietrech. Frank appeared to have an especially intense relationship with Marilyn Maxwell, starting in 1939 and lasting through 1945. But Frank's affair with the famous actress Lana Turner took up the most space in the newspapers of the time.

Frank and Lana had met in 1940 when Frank was still with the Dorsey band. Lana, a young woman who had rocketed to stardom largely because of her good looks, kept the press busy as a twenty-one-year-old starlet who dated many musicians and Hollywood A-listers, which led to two marriages and two divorces within a short time. At first, the relationship between Lana and Frank seems to have been platonic in nature; and Nancy, Frank's wife, claimed to be friendly with Lana socially. However, by 1946 Lana and Frank had begun an intimate affair that was barely concealed from the press. In October, Frank's publicist Evans publicly announced that Frank had separated from Nancy. Frank attributed his marital problems to "constant squabbling," but everyone knew that Frank had been seen at Lana's Palm Springs apartment.

This affair posed a serious publicity problem for MGM Studios. Both Frank and Land had contracts with MGM. At the time, actors' and musicians' contracts with major studios included a morals clause. This reflected the power of popular opinion of the time that immoral behavior by stars was unacceptable, which could lead to a drop in popularity and, thus, in revenue for the studio. MGM swooped in and forced Lana to make a public announcement that there was no affair going on with Frank.

Frank, for his part, had an elaborate reunion with Nancy seventeen days after separating from her and told reporters that he was going back home to his wife and children.

Philanderer that Frank was, he seemed to suffer from guilt. He became ill after the separation and reunion with Nancy, and he was reported to be on the brink of a nervous breakdown. His temper began to flare again, and he made more angry threats to reporters and journalists. He was voted "the least cooperative star of the year" by Hollywood Women's Press Club. MGM confirmed that Frank was too ill to shoot his latest movie.

But neither the affair nor the marriage ended as a result of Frank's discomfort or the MGM executives' efforts. Lana reported to friends that she and Frank were truly in love, and friends assisted them in continuing to meet up. However, Frank stayed married to Nancy for another four years.

Marilyn Maxwell in Brief

Blonde bombshell Marvel Marilyn Maxwell was born August 3, 1921 (some accounts give different years). She started out as a teenager on radio but soon signed with MGM to become a star of the silver screen.

Marilyn Maxwell's curves and good looks had people comparing her to Marilyn Monroe. Marilyn's success, however, was more varied. She appeared in many films but also continued to sing on the radio and performed on television. Marilyn appeared frequently with Bob Hope on tour, and it was rumored that the two had a long-term affair.

Marilyn married three times and had one son. Her son discovered her body in 1972. An autopsy determined that she had a heart attack.

Chapter 12: The Beginning of the Fall

Although, later in life, Frank referred to his trip to Cuba with Luciano and other mobsters as "one of the dumbest things he ever did," he quickly added to the list of potential winners of that title. Many things in Frank's life, which was already fraying at the edges, began to fall apart spectacularly, at least partly due to his own poor decisions.

Before leaving for Havana, Frank had learned that Nancy was pregnant. Nancy told him that she was considering having an abortion, but Frank never took her seriously since abortion was both illegal and strictly against Nancy's Catholic beliefs. He failed to recognize her seriousness and was later shocked when he learned that she had completed the abortion.

Frank's acting career was also flopping. Three of his movies in a row had not done well in the box office. Worst of all, Frank's musical career was not thriving: he only had one top single in the year 1948; and for the first time in six years, he was not voted one of America's top three singers.

Meanwhile, Frank was working as hard as ever on his music, perfecting the art of enunciating every word in his songs, a skill that came to be known as phrasing. He returned to his old singing coach in Hoboken. But the quality of the music that he produced was erratic, vacillating from highly original, stunning hits to poor-quality flops. Biographers attribute

Frank's mixed musical success at this time to his estrangement from his audience. The young teenage swooners who had screamed for him had grown up, and the women they became did not like Frank's philandering ways. Then the United States entered into the Cold War and the Korean War, reminding audiences that Sinatra had never served in the military. To make matters worse, he was suspected of being a communist or a communist supporter.

Frank's family life also continued to fall apart. He got into a fight with his mother Dolly over finances, and the two did not speak for the following two years. During that time, Frank's grandfather Francesco passed away. While Frank and Nancy kept up the charade of the happy couple at their Toluca Home estate in Los Angeles and their new vacation home in Palm Springs, Frank continued his philandering ways. When Nancy became pregnant again in 1947, his publicists used the news to dispel rumors of continuing marital trouble.

At age thirty-three, Frank began to withdraw from his family and the public. He told a friend that he felt finished and used up.

Chapter 13: Frank Sinatra, Mr. Gardner

Some of Frank's friends believe that the real demise of Frank Sinatra came in the form of Ava Gardner. Ava was a beautiful, unknown actress from North Carolina, who gained notoriety early in her career for her well-publicized love affairs with famous men, including actor Mickey Rooney, wealthy movie producer Howard Hughes, and musician Artie Shaw. She was briefly married to both Rooney and Shaw. Her most famous—and infamous—qualities were her unbelievable beauty, her short temper and tendency toward violent rage, her love of alcohol, and her crude speech.

Frank and Ava met when she was married to Rooney and again when she was married to Shaw. Frank had commented on her beauty. In 1949, with many other parts of his life falling apart, Frank began to pursue Ava passionately and recklessly. Both of them enjoyed drink, were passionate liberals, and loved music. They soon believed themselves to be in love.

Frank's relationship with Ava was fraught with unhealthy behaviors from the beginning. Early on, they were arrested for shooting out streetlights. Their booze-filled fights were violent and legendary. Both of them were insanely jealous—and with good reason. They frequently cheated on each other, and Frank was in fact still married to Nancy. When photographers took photos of Frank with Ava, he reacted violently, further earning himself a reputation for having a nasty temper. With her husband publicly photographed with another woman on his arm, Nancy finally filed for separation but made it clear to the judge that she did not yet want a divorce.

Meanwhile, Frank's drinking and smoking increased, and he started taking medications to relax. He continued his insecure and alcohol-filled relationship with Ava Gardner. One night, after a fight with Ava, he fired a gun at himself but hit his mattress. He lost his contracts with both MGM and the Music Corporation of America (MCA).

Worst of all, Frank literally lost his voice; in the spring of 1950, he suffered a hemorrhage of his vocal cords and was ordered not to use his voice for the following forty days. Frank claimed to obey the doctor's orders, but press coverage indicates that he flew to Spain in jealous pursuit of Ava, who was filming a movie there and getting very chummy with a co-star. Frank made a fool of himself by screaming at reporters that Ava was not in any romantic relationship with the other actor, a claim that soon became easy to refute as Ava admitted to dating the Spanish celebrity. Frank returned to New York, crushed, and Ava went back to California. MGM officials, now heavily invested in Ava, encouraged their separation. Ava began claiming that she would not be involved with Frank while he was still married.

In 1951, for the first time in many years, Frank did not have any hits on Billboard's list of top songs for the year. He did two radio shows and a CBS TV show, but all were short-lived and brought him little fame. New singers, including Frankie Lane and Eddie Fisher, were far ahead of Frank in popularity. According to friends, Frank tried to kill himself by putting his head in a gas stove after being jeered at by some fans of Eddie Fisher. Frank was revived. Meanwhile, Ava Gardner was receiving more and more fame and publicity.

In the summer of 1950, Nancy announced that she was seeking a divorce. Frank began taking as many live singing gigs as he could, likely to make money, as his records were no longer selling and his movie career seemed to be over. He and Ava continued their jealous and all-consuming relationship. In August of 1951, after learning that Ava had indeed slept with the Spanish actor for whom she had claimed to have no feelings months before, Frank took too many sleeping pills and had to get his stomach pumped.

Shortly afterward, Ava Gardner was rumored to have had an abortion. MGM officials rushed to get Frank and Ava married before their relationship could cause any more bad publicity. Ava called the marriage off at one point, but the couple ended up wedding on November 7, 1951, in Philadelphia. Frank reportedly screamed and cursed at the press gathered outside. The pair rushed off to Miami and then to Cuba, where they continued to fight.

By early 1952, the press was referring to Frank as "Mr. Gardner" to poke fun at the fact that his career was failing while Ava's was rocketing. To make matters worse, Frank's female fans had now largely turned against him, disapproving of his marriage to Ava and desertion of Nancy.

Frank and Ava both had reputations of being extremely nasty towards the press; Frank and his bodyguards destroyed one cameraman's film and damaged his camera, and Frank was rumored to have threatened to run over a photographer in LA. The press began to ignore him, which made his fall to obscurity even quicker. Frank eventually wrote a penitent article to members of the press in *American Weekly*.

As a married couple, Frank and Ava acted no less insecure and erratic than they had as a couple having an affair. Ava constantly accused Frank of cheating, even while she herself had affairs, including with John Farrow, the director of one of the movies that she was in.

During an infamous fight in October 1952, Frank stormed out of the house, announcing to Ava that he was going to go have sex with Lana Turner, who was staying at his Palm Springs condo while making a movie. Ava sped off after him in the night. A drunken fracas followed, with rumors swirling that Frank had had sex with both or either of the women at the Palm Springs house, or that Lana and Ava were discovered having sex with each other. The fight ended with Frank packing up his things and storming off to a friend's house.

In response, Ava changed her phone number and refused to speak to Frank. Frank went to a journalist, whom he asked to write about how much Frank loved Ava and would do anything to get her back—a pathetic move for a man who proclaimed hatred for the paparazzi. Soon Ava and Frank were seen together again at a rally for a Democratic presidential candidate.

As Frank began to get booed off stages of half-filled theaters and clubs, even on his home turf of New Jersey and New York, Ava landed a role in a huge movie called *Mogambo*, filmed in Kenya. Frank, broke and out of work, accompanied Ava to Kenya for the filming. The couple continued their unhealthy rampages there, and Ava, who had become pregnant before leaving the States, flew to London for an abortion without Frank knowing about the pregnancy. Cast and crewmembers at the Kenya site reported that Ava treated Frank dismissively, as if he were an annoying brother, and wouldn't allow him into the filming area. When Frank arranged an elaborate Christmas surprise for Ava in which he sang Christmas carols for the whole camp, she seemed at first to jeer at him, before realizing how special everyone else thought the gesture.

Frank's only hope for his career now shone from an opportunity to play a part in the movie *From Here to Eternity*. The role for which he was auditioning—that of Maggio, a skinny Italian American kid in the army, who was bullied by his higher-ranking officers—felt personal to him. He was competing with several other actors for the role, however, and felt depressed about his chances of landing it.

Meanwhile, Ava entered into an affair with a rich hunter on the set, a famed romancer of women. Ava became pregnant around that time but flew again to London for an abortion, possibly because she did not know with whose child she was pregnant. Frank did know about this pregnancy and was upset about the abortion. Perhaps because he found out about the affair with the hunter, Frank and Ava had a huge, public fight at a high-end party in Nairobi.

Frank was eventually offered and accepted the role of Maggio in *From Here to Eternity*, although for a low fee. Frank and costar Montgomery Clift began filming in Hawaii and took to getting extremely drunk together every night. Although Ava still claimed to the newspapers to want to have children with Frank, she and Frank filed for separation in October of 1953.

Three weeks later, Frank tried to commit suicide yet again by slashing one of his wrists. He began to see a psychiatrist. He had lost an unhealthy amount of weight and was beginning to bald. Frank and his publicists glossed over the suicide-attempt story to the press, and Frank appeared on a television show, with scars on his wrist, on November 29, 1953.

Montgomery Clift in Brief

Montgomery Clift was born on October 17, 1920, along with a twin sister. Although starting his acting career in the theater, Montgomery began starring in movies in his twenties, after many years of rejecting movie scripts. In Hollywood his good looks and skilled acting provided him with many roles. He was especially known for his roles as the brooding leading man, much like James Dean. He was nominated for multiple Oscars.

His personal life was troubled. In addition to suffering physical ailments both small and large, he had trouble with drug addiction. Montgomery's personal difficulties were aggravated by having to hide his sexuality from the public. As a gay man in 1950s Hollywood, he was forced to play up friendships with women for the public. Gossip frequently linked him with Elizabeth Taylor.

In 1957 he crashed his car after leaving one of Elizabeth Taylor's parties. Montgomery was hospitalized and underwent reconstructive surgery. This accident is sometimes blamed for the drug addiction that plagued him. Montgomery Clift continued to act after the accident, but in 1966 he died suddenly of a heart attack.

Chapter 14: Frank Has a Little Help from His Friends

Biographers refer to these dark years in Frank's personal and professional life as "The Fall," referring to a fall from fame that is essential to the story of many legendarily famous people. Part of the magic of the story is that the hero must have the strength to get up after having fallen, itself a heroic act. However, plenty of evidence points to the fact that Frank did not pick himself up out of this professional and personal hole; rather, he had the help of some very influential friends in the Mob.

At a time when Frank could not get work elsewhere, he found it in Mob-controlled clubs and casinos around the country that had a financial interest in him. A multitude of evidence points to the likelihood that the Mob got Frank the role in *From Here to Eternity* through threats, a scenario that is portrayed in Mario Puzo's book *The Godfather.* In that book, a character who closely resembles Frank Sinatra begs a Mafia don to get him a role in a movie so that he can get back on top in the music and film industry. The don complies and, in a famous scene, places a horse's head in the movie studio producer's bed as a none-too-veiled threat of what could happen if the character is not given the desired part. The studio executive in the movie closely resembles Harry Cohn, the head of the studio in charge of *From Here to Eternity*; and while Cohn didn't own horses, he loved the racetrack and did have a favorite horse. While no horses appeared to have been killed in the real-life version of the story, Cohn somehow received a clear message about what would happen to him if he did not cast Frank in the movie. He complied.

The Mob's financial interest in Frank centered on his ability to bring crowds into the casinos they ran in Las Vegas and other cities. Frank was soon ensconced as a major attraction in Las Vegas's Sands Hotel, a connection he kept for the rest of his life. To protect their investment in Frank, the Mob also became involved in Frank's personal life. Early on, high-ranking mobsters encouraged Frank to stay with his wife; a family man in their culture had a mistress but did not flaunt her in public to the embarrassment of the family. A lawyer for the Mob notified his colleagues of Frank's wrist-slashing episode, and an agent was assigned to stay with Frank for a period following the emergency.

Frank's connection to the Mob wasn't only protective in nature. Frank ran the risk of failing to keep up his end of the bargain. Other singers and actors who were similarly assisted by the Mob met untimely ends when they didn't show up for performances arranged by the Mob or otherwise crossed Mob agents. Frank seemed to admire and emulate the Mob, dressing in dark clothes and adopting their speech, and he sought acting roles in which he played mobsters. However, his irresponsibility in failing to show up to performances and otherwise offending Mob bosses was risky and could have led to his demise.

In August 1953, *From Here to Eternity* opened in movie theaters to great aplomb. Frank's acting was praised, and he won an Oscar for his role as Maggio in March of 1954. Around that time, Frank's voice began to come back in all of its strength. Frank was on his way back up.

Chapter 15: Frank Sinatra, the Turbulent

Frank Sinatra once described himself to the press as bipolar. His medical evaluation for the army reflected that he struggled with anxiety and instability. Numerous friends spoke of the palpable air of tension and restlessness that surrounded Frank. On the set of one movie, he was nicknamed after a prescription medication that gave people energy. He was renowned for his obsession with cleanliness and orderliness in his personal belongings, which was reflected in his impeccable dress and demand for the finest, cleanest household linens and goods. He did not like to be touched by strangers. In the course of his lifetime, he made at least three suicide attempts.

Tina Sinatra described her father as a man who deeply needed love but who couldn't connect emotionally with other people. Perhaps this explains the power dynamic many people observed between Frank and his friends: he demanded total loyalty and cut friends by whom he felt betrayed completely out of his life. To be his friend was, as one of his songs said, a matter of "all or nothing at all." When a friend was hurt, sick, or down and out, Frank was at the friend's side loyally and consistently; but if Frank perceived that a friend even mildly breached Frank's trust, that friend could be threatened, screamed at, and cut off completely. Many people who knew Frank well echoed the sentiment that Frank could be the most generous person in the world or the most selfish and cruel, depending on the circumstances.

Frank's legendary hair-trigger temper was often demonstrated by violence, either perpetrated by himself or by the loyal "heavyweights" who stayed near his side. In one particularly brutal incident in June of 1966, Frank and companion Dean Martin injured a fellow diner at the Beverly Hill Hotel so severely that the man entered a coma and needed brain surgery. The man had made the mistake of asking Frank and his eight companions to quiet down.

Comedian Jackie Mason responded to Frank's heckling during a show by calling him a "middle-aged juvenile delinquent." Mason was rewarded by having shots fired at his window and, soon after, his nose broken by one of Frank's heavyweights. Mason was threatened that much worse could happen to those who crossed Frank Sinatra.

In a well-documented incident, Frank returned to a parking garage after almost being hit by a car driven by a parking attendant earlier. A large bodyguard accompanied him. The two men beat up three parking employees. The bodyguard served ten days in prison and Frank settled out of court on charges of assault and battery. Frank used his own fists to beat up individuals he felt disrespected him, including comedian Shecky Greene and a casino employee who did not believe that the Frank he spoke with on the phone was Mr. Frank Sinatra. In 1964 Frank punched a hotel owner after being told the kitchen was closed when he demanded food at one in the morning. The hotel owner had come to apologize to Frank with a bottle of champagne.

When Frank threatened Sands casino vice-president Carl Cohen in the fall of 1967, he got a taste of his own medicine. The Sands had always been Frank's stomping grounds, where he was treated like royalty due to his Mafia connections (see chapters 9 and 18). However, Howard Hughes, an enemy of Frank's due to their mutual romantic entanglement with Ava Gardner, became the new owner of the Sands, and Frank's credit was denied. At the moment of the denial, Frank went meekly home. He showed up at the hotel later, crashing through a plate-glass window in a golf cart, throwing chairs, ruining furniture, and trying to set the place on fire.

Frank was convinced to go home to Palm Springs; but the next day, again drinking heavily, he returned to the Sands demanding to see Cohen, who was asleep. Cohen emerged to meet Frank at six in the morning, and Frank overturned a table on him. Cohen was a large, well-connected man and one of the few people in town who would not tolerate Frank's behavior. Cohen punched Frank, knocking out his two front teeth. Frank left town but turned to his Mafia friends to take revenge. However, his Mafia friends told him to drop the issue and failed to come to his defense. After the incident, Frank immediately severed his contract with the Sands and signed a new one with Caesar's Palace, another huge Vegas casino.

Frank's drinking likely contributed to his violent outbursts. Friends reported that when Frank was bored and liquored up, he would go out looking for fights. Those who knew Frank well knew to get out of the way when Frank had had too much to drink. By the 1960s, Frank's drinking had become a disturbingly entrenched part of his life. Frank joked about his alcohol use, and some friends claim that his constant drinking of Jack Daniels was actually a publicity stunt—that, in truth, he talked more about drinking than he actually drank. Others, however, recalled Frank's disturbing ability to drink an entire bottle of Jack Daniels in one sitting and remembered that while Frank rarely appeared inebriated in public, in private he frequently showed signs of extreme drunkenness. Alcoholism likely ran in Frank's family, and Frank's high tolerance for alcohol and his violent mood-shifts while drinking were telltale signs of alcohol dependence and abuse.

Although Frank claimed that he would never hurt a woman, his many relationships with women were not free from allegations of violence. While some of Frank's lovers recalled Frank as sweet and tender, others described him as demanding and pushy. Zsa Zsa Gabor claimed that Frank had pushed his way into her house and refused to leave until she had sex with him, which she eventually did so that he would leave before her daughter woke up. Zsa Zsa claimed that Frank tried to force himself on her again years later, during his marriage to Mia Farrow.

An aspiring actress named Sandra Giles claimed that one night after drinking with Frank and a crowd of friends, she woke up naked in his bed. Frank claimed that they had already had sex, but Sandra was sure that they had not and that his claim was a trick to get her to do so. Six months after Frank's divorce from Mia Farrow, Susan Murphy, a woman with whom Frank had flown to Vegas one night on a date, reported that Frank had forced her to have sex after Susan had clearly refused. After, Frank expected her to stay with him. Susan didn't tell anyone for quite a while afterward, convinced that no one would believe her. She stated that Frank acted as though he thought he was a god and could do anything that he wanted with impunity.

A hatcheck girl in a Hollywood restaurant claimed that Frank threw her through a plate-glass window when she refused to consent to his sexual demands, which required her to get numerous stitches. When Frank's wife Mia turned up at the set of a movie covered in bruises, rumors swirled that Frank had physically abused her, although both Frank and Mia denied these allegations.

Many people close to Frank reported that Frank seemed to see women as objects to be used for sex and then discarded. An aspiring actress, Shirley Van Dyke, had a long-running relationship in which Frank helped get her acting roles in exchange for sex. Van Dyke attempted suicide and mentioned being hurt by Frank in some of her suicide notes. Actress Eva Bartok became pregnant by Frank but didn't bother telling him about the pregnancy since she did not believe the two would be a successful couple. However, she appealed to Frank to reach out to his daughter, Deana, who knew Frank was her father and wanted to meet him. Frank ignored Eva's pleas and responded through his attorney that he was too busy to meet Deana. When Deana herself reached out to Frank as an adult, begging him to respond to her, he similarly ignored her letter.

One of Frank's longer-term girlfriends, Peggy Connelly, who dated Frank while he was in his early forties, described Frank as very close-mouthed about his feelings. According to his daughter Tina, Frank was determined never to get hurt again in the way that Ava had hurt him. Peggy recalled that Frank loved to read and that he was ashamed of his lack of education. Peggy described Frank as always tense and on the move, always thinking about being somewhere else. Peggy saw Frank's dark rages and self-indulgent, selfish behavior at the studio and on the movie set, especially when he engaged in a childish battle with Marlon Brando while working on the set of *Guys and Dolls* with him. She also later acknowledged that Frank hosted Mafia guests from time to time and that he seemed to admire them. As a lover, Peggy described Frank as energetic and engaged but more interested in his own pleasure than his partner's.

Frank was especially notorious for his violence towards the press. In April 1947 Frank reportedly pulled up to an LA club through a back entrance, entered the club, and began beating up a reporter named Lee Mortimer with the help of three men, obviously brought with him for that purpose. Mortimer had written negative columns about Frank, but the two had never spoken directly. The following day, Frank was arrested for assault and battery. He managed to settle the case for a great deal of money, but Mortimer's newspaper chain, the large and powerful Hearst Company, made special efforts to focus on Frank's shady behavior with the Mob and the suspicions that he was a communist.

The bad press might have continued indefinitely if Frank didn't make the rare move of going directly to the head of the Hearst chain of newspapers, William Hearst, and humbling himself. Nonetheless, in 1958 Frank was accused of trying to run down a photographer who refused to call Frank "Mr. Sinatra." In 1964 Frank was arrested in Spain for a violent tussle with reporters, and he tossed cherry bombs at reporters in France later that same year, causing car accidents and injuries. Many reporters who encountered Frank recalled his brutal threats and his constant accompaniment by heavyweights who did not hesitate to inflict physical damage.

Frank's reputation for violence was tempered by his known generosity. He performed for free for a club owner's widow in order to save her from financial ruin. He paid others' hospital bills, including those of pianist Bill Miller, Buddy Rich, and Mabel Mercer. When Joe Louis had a stroke, Frank arranged and paid for top-notch care. He rescued Billie Holiday from a psychiatric unit of a public hospital and paid for her care in a private ward until her death. He paid for his own fees on a World Tour For Children, raising millions of dollars for children's causes.

He also showed generosity to non-famous persons, paying for the medical care of his hotel maid's husband, hiring an attorney to help an elderly couple facing eviction, and sending food and money to children who had suffered accidents. According to close friends, his generosity seemed to be invoked spontaneously in response to seeing sad events on the news and in his everyday life and it may have been motivated partially by his Italian culture, which emphasized the value of being the *padrone*, or the man who provides for the townspeople in return for their respect and obedience.

Zsa Zsa Gabor in Brief

Frank's long and difficult history with women intertwined his story with that of many famous actresses, including Zsa Zsa Gabor. She was born in Hungary on February 6, 1917 to a wealthy family. Zsa Zsa attended boarding school, then acting school. By the age of fifteen, she had already performed on stage and married.

Zsa Zsa's sister Eva went to America and married. Zsa Zsa and their mother joined Eva in America after they both divorced. There, Zsa Zsa married and divorced again within a few years. This time the marriage produced a daughter.

In the 1950s, Zsa Zsa began appearing in movies and on television, becoming famous quickly. Her looks and her personality made her a Hollywood favorite. Zsa Zsa's personal life, with many marriages and even more money, made her a tabloid favorite. In 1989 she served three days in prison for slapping a police officer, a scandal of much interest to the public.

She is currently married to Prince Frederick von Anhalt. This union officially makes the vivacious actress a princess.

Chapter 16: Frank Sinatra, Remade and Looking for Love

In April 1953, Frank began an alliance with a new arranger, named Nelson Riddle. With Nelson, Frank recorded many of the albums that made him a legend. Biographers consider the work that Frank produced with Nelson to have launched him into a second career that was even more glorious than his first. With Nelson Riddle, Frank remade himself—he not only changed clothes, movie studios, and record studios, but he also changed the way that he sang. Stepping away from the romantic crooning that he had performed as a young man, he infused the songs that he sang with rich notes of pain and meaning. Deeper, darker, and fuller, these songs almost all included a theme of loneliness. Together, Nelson and Frank made a brand name of loneliness and, in doing so, won a new audience: men. Frank's great strength of being able to connect with audiences in an intimate way came through to a generation of men struggling with loneliness and rejection.

While dealing with painful themes, Nelson's style was by no means heavy-handed or melancholy. His sound was upbeat and fresh, and Frank heard in it the classic music and jazz that he had grown up worshipping. Frank praised Nelson as the greatest arranger in the world but maintained a high degree of musical control on the records. Nelson described Frank's ability to infuse life into lyrics and impeccable taste as unparalleled. The duo's combined talent led to nine albums over as many years, many of which have become embedded in the nation's musical and cultural collective memory.

Now presenting a more refined, worn image, Frank appealed to the public as a hero who had fallen and fought his way back. He increasingly wore hats, likely to cover up his baldness, and his hat and suit became his trademark style. In private, he often wore the color orange, and he bought orange décor for his home.

Frank's success at infusing loneliness into his singing was not entirely due to an ability to feign emotion. He was still pining over Ava Gardner. He and Ava were still legally married and got together occasionally over the next few years, with Frank making it clear that he wanted Ava back. Ava, on the other hand, claimed to others that she was through with Frank; yet she still agreed to see him and traveled with a collection of his records.

When the two did get together, however, they quickly fell back into their screaming fights. Frank filled his Los Angeles residence with pictures of Ava and of the two of them together. Friends and neighbors reported that he would alternatively cry in front of these images and smash them. He bought a life-sized nude statue of Ava that had been made for a scene in her movie *The Barefoot Contessa* and installed it in his garden. On the night that he won his Oscar for *From*

Here to Eternity, Frank was found by police wandering alone in Beverly Hills, likely wishing that Ava Gardner were present to share his proud accomplishment.

Frank still visited Nancy and his growing children and gave conflicting stories about whether he wished that he had stayed in the marriage to Nancy or was glad that he had left. He told the press that he would not discuss his personal life anymore. There was plenty to discuss, however. Frank continued his womanizing ways, fooling some women into believing he actually wanted a marriage with them. Frank himself seemed confused on the topic.

For a brief time, he dated Gloria Vanderbilt, a millionaire heiress who was married to an elderly conductor. While the romance was short-lived, many attributed his reference to "blue-blooded girls of independent means" in "It was a Very Good Year" to this relationship with Gloria. Frank also dated the young actresses Jill Corey and Anita Ekberg, and he continued his old fling with Marilyn Dietrich.

Frank's private life during this very successful period of his career seemed to involve loneliness, disengagement, and a lot of alcohol. He slept with women and dumped them if there was any emotional connection. He withdrew from many friends. He had violent confrontations with journalists. He moved into a new house in an isolated, beautiful location in Beverly Hills, where he was seen alone many nights with his telescope. Frank's refuges from his loneliness included the home of Nancy and the children, where he would wind up asleep on the couch, and times spent with famous friends at his Palm Springs home.

Jeanne Carmen, a model and burlesque star, continued an on-and-off relationship with Frank for seven years starting in the mid-1950s. She described him as sad and needy, always pining away for Ava Gardner. Frank proposed marriage several times to Jeanne, but Jeanne was aware that Frank had a split mind about marriage and was just looking for stability.

Frank managed to sustain a long relationship with a young singer named Peggy Connelly. A newcomer to Hollywood, Peggy was in her early twenties and Frank thirty-nine when they met in 1955. Peggy was a relatively naïve girl from the South when she met Frank, and Frank opened doors for her that she had never imagined. She found herself spending time with the most famous stars in Hollywood and dining and staying at the finest establishments. Peggy maintained a relationship with Frank for almost three years, from 1955 to 1957.

Frank's movie career was taking off, and he was releasing music that made him a legend, including "I Got You Under

My Skin" "and "You Make Me Feel So Young." Between 1955 and 1957, during Peggy's relationship with Frank, he starred in *Guys and Dolls, The Tender Trap,* and *High Society*. He also starred in, and was nominated for an Oscar for his performance in, *The Man with the Golden Arm*, though to his sore disappointment, he did not win.

While Peggy chose to be faithful to Frank, she made no such demands on him and suffered no disillusions about his womanizing ways. When Peggy and Frank went to Spain so Frank could film *The Pride and the Passion*, they had many uncomfortable collisions with Ava Gardner. Ava was often present at the restaurant where the couple dined, and she would rush out in tears when she saw Peggy and Frank arrive. Peggy could see that Frank wanted to be with Ava and was not surprised to return to their hotel suite after a trip to find Ava there in Frank's bathrobe. Frank and Ava did not apologize or explain.

When Frank returned to the United States, Ava announced that she was finalizing her divorce to Frank and possibly marrying a new boyfriend. Around that time, Frank proposed to Peggy for the first time. Peggy wisely declined; and when Frank proposed again later in the year, she finally realized that she would not be able to live with Frank's womanizing ways and use of prostitutes, and she broke it off with him. Ava sued Frank for divorce shortly afterwards.

Around the time of his divorce from Ava and breakup with Peggy, Frank was spending a lot of time with his famous friends Humphrey Bogart and Lauren Bacall, Bogart's wife, along with other Hollywood stars including Judy Garland, John Huston, and Katherine Hepburn. Humphrey and Lauren, who had been married for nine years, welcomed friends into their home and lavishly entertained both there and on Humphrey's boat. Humphrey was fifty-four and Frank thirty-eight when they met, but the two seemed to have much in common: both were drinkers who liked to play the role of the tough guy. However, the two did not have a close friendship beyond drinking together, as Humphrey was frequently annoyed by Frank's extravagant lifestyle and constant self-indulgence. Humphrey may have had another reason to dislike Frank—he resented the special connection Frank had with his wife Lauren. However, when Humphrey became ill with throat cancer in 1956, Frank showed himself to be an extremely loyal and steadfast friend, constantly trying to cheer up Humphrey.

Lauren Bacall, who was twenty-five years younger than her husband, claimed that she never strayed during her marriage to Humphrey. Shortly before Humphrey died, there was talk of a relationship between Lauren and Frank. After Humphrey passed away of his illness, Frank and Lauren began to spend an abundance of time together, and Frank proposed to Lauren. However, when she didn't answer, he became angry, and the two didn't talk for a month. When they reunited, Frank once again proposed, and this time Lauren accepted.

However, when the press asked Frank about the proposal, he became enraged and accused Lauren of having told the press about it. The accusation didn't make much sense since Lauren had already told Frank about the news story and both of them had shared their news with a mutual friend, who was an agent of the press. Frank cut off all communication with Lauren, going so far as to ignore her at dinner parties at mutual friends' houses. Lauren, humiliated at the time, later felt relief that she didn't marry Frank. As she and other friends admitted, his treatment of her was horrible, and he soon would have strayed.

During Frank's comeback period, the nation was humming about a new music sensation called rock-and-roll, personified in the form of Elvis Presley and his gyrating pelvis. Frank deplored "rock 'n' roll" as vile and dirty, clearly insecure about his position in a changing music scene. He needn't have worried; his songs continued to top the charts, and his album *Only the Lonely* was the bestselling album for two and a half years. He also was starring in many successful movies and was voted top male singer by the annual *Down Beat* polls. The use of his image in ads for cigarettes and watches alone netted him millions of dollars.

Dean Martin in Brief

On June 7, 1917, Dino Crocetti, later Dean Martin, was born. His early career included jobs such as bootlegging and card dealing. One fateful day, his friends convinced him to sing on stage, and Dean was hooked. Luckily, he had a good voice, too. Dean began singing more and more, ending up in nightclubs in New York.

In the city, he met Jerry Lewis, and the famous duo was formed. Dean was the heartthrob and Jerry the comic relief. Their act made it to radio, television, and film. They split up in 1956.

Around this time, Dean began performing with the Rat Pack. He fit right in with Frank Sinatra. They both had an Italian heritage, a love of alcohol, and terrible relationships with women.

Dean had three marriages, with four children from the first marriage. He performed until 1989, when illness took him off tour. He died December 25, 1995.

Chapter 17: The Rat Pack

As Frank's career soared, his personal life was, as always, tumultuous. He continued to pursue Ava, who would reunite with him for a few days and then leave again. His brief relationships with models and actresses were quickly over, and he began to frequent prostitutes even more often. Perhaps as an answer to his loneliness, Frank undertook the formation of a "club" of rule-breakers, famous men and women with plenty of money and a disdain for social norms. The group became the ultimate cult of personality for Frank Sinatra.

This club got the name "Rat Pack" when Lauren Bacall saw the group together, hung-over after days of debauchery in Las Vegas, and remarked that they looked like a rat pack. The Pack came together while Frank and fellow members were filming a movie called *Some Came Running* in a small town in Indiana. Frank and Dean Martin co-starred in the movie, in which a young Shirley MacLaine also had an important role. The two men made headlines for their bad behavior in the small town, drinking, carousing, and making fun of locals. The Rat Pack came to include Peter Lawford, Joey Bishop, and Sammy Davis Jr. The crew even developed their own lingo and nicknames for each other.

Dean Martin had a lot in common with Frank: both were Italian high-school dropouts, had been born into poor immigrant families, and liked drinking and women. Dean was a singer and an actor who eventually made his mark performing with Jerry Lewis and singing the famous songs "That's Amore" and "Memories Are Made of This." Dean's second wife described Dean as being unreachable, always remote from friends, so even while he and Sinatra remained friends, Dean was inaccessible to Frank as a close crony.

Frank's relationship with Sammy Davis Jr. had all the hallmarks of Frank's personality—extreme loyalty, mercurial swings, and an obsessive need to be obeyed. Sammy Davis Jr. was a young black actor and performer whom Frank discovered early in Sammy's career. Frank supported Sammy by getting him gigs he otherwise could not have gotten as a young black man at the time. When Sammy was badly injured in a car accident in 1954, blinding him in one eye, Frank supported him through his recuperation.

Frank also helped Sammy get out of a sticky situation with the Mafia. When Sammy began dating white actress Kim Novak, studio boss Harry Cohn called in a favor with the Mob, who made it clear to Sammy what would happen to a black man, however famous, who came near a white star. Frank served as the mediator between Sammy and the Mob, and soon Sammy married an unknown black woman in an arrangement made with the Mob to show that he would not pursue Novak.

While Sammy reportedly worshipped Frank, the two did not always get along perfectly. Frank became extremely jealous when he saw a picture of his friend with Ava Gardner, and Sammy further infuriated Frank by telling the press that Frank at times treated people inexcusably badly. The two publicly reconciled when Sammy apologized in front of the audience at a charity performance, and they continued their friendship.

Peter Lawford, who became known as Rat Pack member "Charley the Seal," was a British actor who became well known in the States for his charming good looks. He idolized Frank but had a predictably mercurial relationship with him. Frank caught wind that Peter had gone on a date with Ava, which was likely only a rumor, and called Peter in the middle of the night to curse him out and threaten him. Frank refused to speak to Peter for the next few years, until he inexplicably forgave Peter in 1957. Peter and Frank's biographers believe that Peter's marriage to Senator John F. Kennedy's sister Patricia may have motivated Frank to reconcile with Peter, as Frank undoubtedly saw Peter's political connections as promising. Ultimately, however, the two would part ways again, never to reconcile.

Joey Bishop in Brief

The longest-surviving member of the Rat Pack, Joey Bishop was born February 3, 1918. His birth name was Joseph Abraham Gottlieb, but he later changed his surname to Bishop.

A comedian with a history in television, Bishop was doing stand-up as young as eighteen and continued to be a funnyman his whole life. A small break to fight in World War II did not stop him from pursuing his career in comedy. He was a frequent guest host of *The Tonight Show* in its Johnny Carson heyday and had his own comedy show as well.

Bishop joined the Rat Pack after he became friends with Frank Sinatra. He often performed in Vegas with the rest of the Pack. His nickname was "The Frown Prince" because of his gloomy, sarcastic demeanor and jokes. The fame and influence of the Rat Pack brought Bishop to the big screen. He acted in movies until the 1990s.

Bishop married only once, to Sylvia Ruzga, and had one son from his marriage. This kind of commitment was a rarity amongst his Rat Pack brethren. Bishop outlived his wife by about eight years. He died on October 17, 2007.

Chapter 18: Frank and JFK

In early 1960 the Rat Pack performed a show called "The Summit" at the Sands Hotel in Las Vegas. The show consisted of men of the Rat Pack getting drunk on stage, performing slapstick humor, and singing famous tunes with lyrics altered to make lewd jokes. The show also poked fun at the racist attitudes of the time, with Davis being the butt of or the initiator of jokes about race and racism. The press described the show as a shameless celebration of "men having fun" and "American alcoholism," but the show raked in money as crowds flocked to see the Rat Pack. The Rat Pack, meanwhile, lived extravagant lives in Las Vegas during their tour there, dubbing the hotel's steam room as their "Club House," where they lounged and entertained myriad female guests, mostly prostitutes.

Presidential hopeful John F. Kennedy made an appearance at one of the performances of "The Summit" at the Sands. By then, Frank had already thrown his support behind the candidate, much as he had for Roosevelt. JFK had youthful good looks and a beautiful wife and baby. The world saw him as a very clean-cut, moral young man and a veteran of World War II.

As close comrades of Frank Sinatra came to learn, however, the politician had a lot to hide from the public. First were his medical problems, including Addison's disease and chronic back and intestinal ailments, among other things. Second but no less alarming was his drug habit. JFK used prescription drugs, prescribed and otherwise, and cocaine. Finally, JFK was an insatiable womanizer, sleeping with many women, including prostitutes, while married.

Frank hastened to ensure that JFK got all of the drugs and women he needed when he came to Frank's Palm Springs house, and he worked fervently to get JFK elected. In the beginning, Frank was rewarded by being invited to JFK's celebrity functions. The two clearly had plenty in common. Frank's most important contributions to JFK's elections came in the form of his musical anthems to JFK and his use of his Mafia connections.

JFK's father, Joe Kennedy, had a long history of doing business with the Mafia, stemming from his days importing liquor during Prohibition. When his son John decided to run for the Presidency, though, Joe Kennedy sold his interest in the liquor business and turned his powerful will to getting JFK elected. Among his agenda items was making political allies in the Mafia, who controlled many elections across the country. Joe Kennedy paid visits to famous mobster Bill Bonanno in preparation for his son's campaign; but once his son entered the presidential race, Joe couldn't risk dealing directly with the Mafia and having it come back to haunt his son.

For help with the job, Joe Kennedy turned to Frank Sinatra. Frank, as Joe knew, was connected to mobster Sam Giancana, head of the Chicago Mob, whom Joe needed on his side to get the vote for his son in the swing states of Illinois and West Virginia. Sam had several politicians in his pocket as well as several actors and entertainers. While some remembered Sam Giancana as a kind family man, many more recalled his ruthless killings and merciless brutality.

Frank Sinatra agreed, at the urging of Joe Kennedy, to be the intermediary between Sam and the presidential campaign. With Frank's help, JFK won the primary elections in West Virginia and Chicago. Voters were alternatively bribed or threatened into voting for JFK. Frank carried millions of dollars for the operation to the rigged states.

The support of the Mafia nationwide, however, was hard to win; many Mob bosses supported JFK's political rival Lyndon Johnson. The Mob was worried about Congress's recent crackdown on organized crime intensifying under JFK and believed Johnson was more likely to protect their interests. However, Joe Kennedy promised Sam Giancana and other mobsters that their reward for their help with the election would be that his son's administration would relax law enforcement of Mafia activity. Frank repeated these promises, winning over many mobsters.

In addition to throwing parties with multitudes of beautiful actresses and hired prostitutes to satisfy JFK's sexual appetite, Frank also took the additional step of setting him up with Judith Campbell. Evidence points to the likelihood that Judith was a high-end prostitute for the Mob who was given as a gift to JFK. Judith was introduced to JFK at the Sands and continued a sexual relationship with him that lasted into his presidency. Judith was also connected to mobsters Sam Giancana and Rosselli, and she would facilitate meetings between Sam and the politician as well as carry money for the Mafia.

Frank's songs "High Hopes" and "All the Way" became the anthems of JFK's campaign. Frank brought the Rat Pack and other famous entertainers into the work of campaigning for JFK. In addition to having the politician appear at the Sands, Frank arranged for Sammy Davis Jr., Nat King Cole, Ella Fitzgerald, and others to perform at rallies for JFK. Davis postponed his wedding to a white woman until after the election for the purpose of avoiding the negative publicity that it would bring to JFK. Frank and the others raised huge sums of money for JFK's campaign.

Little doubt remains that votes were stolen in Illinois and other parts of the country on election night, catapulting JFK to the top of the popular and electoral vote. The contributing Mafia members waited for their return favors. Exiled mobsters Lucky Luciano and Joe Adonis had hopes of returning from Italy, and Sam Giancana anticipated that the FBI would back off of their investigation of him. They were sorely disappointed, however, when JFK appointed his brother Robert Kennedy as Attorney General. Robert Kennedy set out on a well-publicized agenda to crack down on organized crime. Sam Giancana was bugged and followed extensively by FBI agents, and other mobsters were arrested and deported. Luciano and Adonis remained in exile. The anger of the mobsters for this betrayal began to turn toward their intermediary to President Kennedy and his administration—Frank Sinatra.

The White House and the Kennedy family soon made it clear to Frank that Frank and his Rat Pack were not welcome company for JFK now that he was president. Both Frank and Sammy Davis Jr. were asked not to come to the inauguration even though Frank had been honored privately at a Kennedy function for all of his campaign work and Davis had postponed his own wedding to help the campaign. Frank was asked to make himself less visible and was dis-invited from a vacation that he had planned to take with Joe Kennedy.

The worst slight came when JFK, now president, refused to stay at Frank's house in Palm Springs when visiting the area. Frank had spent a great deal of money outfitting his house to make it ready for President Kennedy, putting in additional phone lines and other luxuries for the president. Not only did JFK decline to stay with Frank, he failed even to stop in at Frank's house. When Frank heard about JFK's change in plans, he threw a violent tantrum, blaming Peter Lawford and permanently severing his friendship with him.

Frank did try to get the new administration to honor its promises to back off from the prosecution of Mafia members, especially Sam Giancana, but his pleas fell on deaf ears. JFK told Frank to speak to his father and Bobby, both of whom refused to take any action to stop the crackdown against the Mob. Instead, Bobby Kennedy went to work deporting as many Italian mobsters as he could and following Sam Giancana's every step. When Joe Kennedy had a stroke in late 1961, Frank lost the last possible ally he had in ensuring that the Kennedy administration would do what Frank had promised the Mob it would do.

Bobby Kennedy wisely chose not to question or implicate Frank Sinatra in his crackdown on organized crime because doing so would likely expose his family's involvement with the Mafia. But Frank faced a much bigger danger—that of being deemed a double-crosser by the Mafia. Sam Giancana had had people killed for far less. One night in Miami, Frank allegedly received a skinned lamb's head, hidden under the silver lid on his room-service tray. According to those who were present, Frank got up, went into his hotel room, and did not leave for the entire day after the none-too-veiled threat.

Frank faced even more danger from Sam Giancana because he was in business with him, the two being co-owners of a Lake Tahoe resort called the Cal-Neva. In reality, Frank was likely a mere front for Sam, the true owner of the casino. People working for Frank recalled large amounts of money being flown into Tahoe from Sam. Now that Sam was under such tight scrutiny, he risked detection by the Nevada Gaming Control Board, which was determined to enforce the rule that Sam Giancana, as a convicted felon, was not to be allowed in any of the state's casinos. Frank snuck him into a secret location in the Cal-Neva anyway and, when investigated by the Board, cursed and threatened Board chairman Ed Olsen. The Board issued a formal complaint against Frank, and Frank was forced to sell his interest in the Cal-Neva to avoid prosecution.

Sam Giancana was not happy. Frank had lost him a lot of money in addition to not keeping his promises about the president. Frank was lucky to be alive; word was that he was only spared from Sam's retribution by the pleas of East Coast mobsters who came to his defense.

JFK was assassinated in Dallas in November of 1963. Soon thereafter, Frank's son, Frankie Jr., was kidnapped while on tour with his own singing group. While the government blamed Kennedy's assassination on a lone, deranged gunman named Lee Harvey Oswald, Jack Ruby, the person who shot Oswald shortly afterward, was heavily involved with the Mafia. To this day, conspiracy theorists believe the Mafia was involved with the killing of JFK.

Frank, for his part, was terrified that his son's abduction and the president's murder were the work of the Mob. Frank continued his relationship with Sam Giancana, but now it was even more fear-based than before, with Sam alternatively socializing with Frank and sending him threats.

Peter Lawford in Brief

Born in England on September 7, 1923, Peter Lawford was the Rat Pack member who was at least as well connected as Frank Sinatra. His father was a knighted veteran and actor, and Lawford himself married into America's version of aristocracy.

Acting by age eight, Lawford was working with MGM by the 1940s. He was married four times, most famously to Patricia Kennedy, sister of John F. Kennedy. They had four children together. Lawford was a leading man in Hollywood. He was good-looking, suave, and experienced.

Lawford had more in common with Frank and Dean than just multiple marriages. He drank heavily and partied with the Pack until he and Frank fought over Robert Kennedy and his anti-Mafia campaign. On December 24, 1984, Peter Lawford died. His excessive use of alcohol is often blamed for his early death.

Chapter 19: Frank Sinatra, the Highest-Paid Man in Hollywood

Frank parted ways with Capital Records in 1962 after the company refused to give him more creative control over his records. He started his own studio, which he named Reprise Records. Frank envisioned himself as a high-powered businessman in this new role, although it is likely that trained professionals handled the majority of the business affairs.

Reprise Records started off shakily and shuddered along until Warner Brothers bought two-thirds of it in 1963. Warner Brothers had offered Frank a very good deal for the company in return for a large portion of Frank's movie profits. Frank starred in nine movies between 1961 and 1965, some starring Rat Pack members Dean Martin and Sammy Davis Jr. Officially, however, the Rat Pack had been disbanded, and the members' movies failed to attract the same huge audiences. All the same, Frank was the highest-paid entertainer in Hollywood at the time. Around this time, Frank starred in *The Manchurian Candidate*, a movie of political intrigue about which Frank was very proud. The movie itself did poorly upon release.

Frank's deal with Warner Brothers greatly increased his fortune. By 1965, he was presiding over Reprise Records in addition to two movie companies, an airplane charter business, and a company that made parts for aircraft and missiles. Frank commuted around California to his many business enterprises on a Leer jet owned by his company. He added onto his Palm Springs home so that it could accommodate his ever-growing staff, and he had a saltwater pool installed. He also rented homes in Beverly Hills and Manhattan. Frank lived extravagantly. Reportedly, he once flew a barber across the country for a haircut.

By 1965, nearing fifty years old and almost completely bald, Frank began talking about retirement. His music reflected his years, both in content and in the lowering of his voice. His hugely popular album *September of My Years* featured songs about aging and reminiscence. As famous as he was, Frank felt threatened by the rock 'n' roll obsession that was sweeping the nation.

At fifty, Frank still continued his incessant pursuit of dozens of women, including prostitutes, non-celebrities, and famous Hollywood stars. This list included, of course, Ava Gardner. Ava, now living in Madrid and sinking into alcoholism, responded to Frank's overtures, and she and Frank continued to meet up in various locations around the world. These visits usually ended in loud drunken fights and Ava storming off. Frank had a longer-than-average relationship with twenty-four year old dancer Juliet Prowse, whom he met on the set of the movie *Can-Can* in 1959, when he was forty-four. Frank and Juliet hit it off, but Frank's hard drinking and possessiveness caused Juliet to reject his marriage proposals. Frank wanted Juliet to accept his womanizing ways while she was expected to remain faithful to him exclusively; and, worse, he expected Juliet to give up her rising career.

During a six-month break with Juliet in 1961, Frank made news by dating Marilyn Monroe. Frank had known Marilyn since she was married to Joe DiMaggio in 1954, and he had reportedly helped DiMaggio try to catch Marilyn in an affair by storming her hotel room. By 1961, Marilyn was nearing the end of her life, taking pills and drinking constantly between periodic hospitalizations for her psychiatric conditions. The affair between Frank and Marilyn seemed relatively serious; but during it, Frank announced his engagement to Juliet, with whom he had reconciled after their separation. Marilyn died shortly afterward.

Frank's engagement to Juliet lasted less than two months. She couldn't tolerate his insistence that she end her career. In October 1964, Frank met his third wife—nineteen-year-old actress Mia Farrow. Ironically, Mia's parents had separated due to Mia's father's affair with Ava Gardner during Mia's childhood. Now a budding actress herself, Mia was known for her childlike innocence and waif-like appearance. She and Frank met at the movie studio Twentieth Century Fox, where Frank invited Mia to travel to Palm Springs on his jet.

Soon the couple was seen many places together, but Frank kept Mia out of his private affairs and did not introduce her to his family for almost a year. Mia clearly did not fit in with Frank's older friends and his Las Vegas casino crew of gangsters and hard-drinking performers. However, after a period of separation, Frank proposed to Mia in the summer of 1966. She accepted. Meanwhile, Frank continued to see Ava whenever he could. After another rejection from Ava in London, Frank called friends and asked them to arrange the marriage with Mia for the following day. Frank and Mia married on July 19, 1966, at the Sands casino in Las Vegas.

The marriage did not last very long. Predictably, the breaking point was over Mia's career, which Frank wanted her to end. When Mia insisted on taking a promising role in the movie *Rosemary's Baby* instead of filming a movie with him in November 1967, he served her with divorce papers. They got divorced a few months later.

Mia Farrow in Brief

Mia Farrow was born into Hollywood. On February 9, 1945, Mia was born to parents John Farrow and Catherine O'Sullivan, both involved in the movie industry. Mia was in movies and on Broadway from a young age but became much better known once *Rosemary's Baby* made its box-office splash.

Her relationship with Frank Sinatra was not her only famous one under the microscope. She later married another man, Andre Previn, and after that divorce became involved with actor and director Woody Allen. The latter relationship famously ended after Farrow discovered that Allen and her adopted daughter were involved in an affair.

Mia Farrow's career is still ongoing, and she has added "activist" to her resume. She focuses on humanitarian efforts and charities.

Chapter 20: Frank in the 1960s

As he entered his mid-fifties, Frank continued as a bachelor and added to his loneliness by breaking ties with many friends. Frank was notorious for disowning friends of several years over what seemed like trivial incidents: he broke off a twenty-five-year friendship with Hank Sanicola over an argument about Frank's involvement with the Mafia; and he fired his valet of fifteen years, George Jacobs, after he found out that George had danced once, at her request, with his ex-wife Mia. Other friends of Frank were dying, many of diseases related to alcohol.

Frank's loyal companion during this time was an Italian American named Jilly Rizzo, a large man with one eye who attempted a career as a prizefighter and later opened a club in Manhattan. The nightclub, called Rizzo's, was Frank's favorite bar, and Rizzo turned it into a living shrine to his friend. Rizzo moved to Palm Springs to be closer to Frank. Frank's daughter Tina remembered the Rizzo became practically part of the family. Rizzo took care of a lot of Frank's dirty work for him, beating up journalists and severely injuring some. Rizzo took the blame when he, Frank, and others beat up a hotel guest in Palm Springs. Rizzo was eventually convicted for fraud for his work connected to the Mafia but was excused from jail time because of his advanced age and poor health.

In 1967 the American Italian Anti-Defamation League, or AID, was founded, with the stated purpose of combating the common negative stereotypes of Italian-Americans as criminals who were all affiliated with the Mafia. Ironically, the League asked Frank Sinatra to be its chairman, an offer he gladly accepted. He performed at a concert in Madison Square Garden to an audience of over eighteen-thousand people. Soon, however, the League was discovered to have several board members with Mafia connections and was disbanded.

The Italian American Civil Rights League (IACRL) quickly replaced AID. Leading mobster Joe Colombo headed the IACRL. Colombo requested that Frank sing at a rally and, when Frank refused, ordered a hit on him. Frank's Mafioso friend Jimmy Alo had to negotiate to get the contract on Frank's life lifted. As a result, Frank agreed to perform at a second concert at Madison Square Garden. However, Frank seemed to be distancing himself from his Mafia connections. He fought a hard legal battle against the producers who were making Mario Puzo's *The Godfather* books into movies, succeeding only in getting the role of the character based on him reduced slightly.

Frank's business with the Mafia was finally catching up with him (see chapters 9, 18, and 20). The FBI bugged his old Mafioso patron Angelo De Carlo's office and recorded De

Carlo discussing his plans to open a casino with Frank. Frank was subpoenaed to testify in New Jersey and found out that he would be jailed for three years if he didn't comply. When Frank appeared, he told his examiners that he had no idea that the men he had dealings with, who were very famous mobsters, had any connection to the Mafia. Frank was also subpoenaed to testify in a Florida court, but he avoided the summons by leaving the state. When the House Select Committee on Crime summoned Frank to appear, he conveniently disappeared to Europe for six weeks. When he finally did appear, he petulantly claimed that he was being questioned due to racial prejudice based on his ethnic background and that he had no connections to organized crime.

Frank's two big hits in the 1960s were "Strangers in the Night" and "My Way." Frank personally detested "Strangers in the Night" as meaningless pop music, but recognized its mass appeal. He also dismissed the notion that "My Way" was in any way autobiographical—although those close to Frank claimed that the anthem of someone defiantly living down all manner of troubles described Frank's style well. Frank released ten albums between 1967 and 1971, but none of them went to the top of the charts. However, Frank's ego got a boost in 1969 when the astronauts aboard the Apollo 10 played Frank's "Fly Me to the Moon" to a listening world.

Frank's father died in 1969, at the age of seventy-four, due to complications from emphysema. Frank mourned his father's death, and Dolly came to live in California near Frank. Predictably, Frank's mother exasperated him with her constant demands. By now, two of Frank's grown children had started careers in music: son Frank Jr. and daughter Nancy had released songs. The mother of Frank's children still supported Frank from the wings, never remarrying.

Chapter 21: Frank, the Retired Republican

In the spring of 1971, Frank began to speak of retiring. Publicly, he said that he was tired of being in the spotlight. Frank's real motivation might have been partly due to fraying protection from his Mafia connections. The Mob had failed to defend him in a recent dispute with an official at the Caesar's Palace casino, and many of his old Mob connections were dead or in jail.

On June 13, 1971, Frank gave what he told the public would be his last performance at the Los Angeles Music Center. Over five-thousand people attended the concert, including famous actors and the vice president of the United States. His last three songs were "Oh, Happy Day," "All or Nothing At All," and "Angel Eyes." Even though he came out onto the stage for an encore to oblige the screaming audience, he declined to sing another song. He told reporters that he was tired.

For many months, Frank didn't sing but devoted himself instead to other efforts, including painting landscapes and abstract pictures. He also took to painting and collecting images of clowns, an interest he claimed was inspired by admiration for the famous clown Emmett Kelly. Frank's daughter Tina saw her father's clown paintings as paintings of himself, a sad man who made serious attempts to do many foolish things.

Frank also began surrounding himself with older, educated friends and seeking women who he felt had class and culture. He found that in Lois Nettleton, an actress whom he began dating in 1971. Lois and Frank dated for about a year, and she reported that she found Frank to be very gallant and charming for the majority of the relationship. Frank even proposed marriage to Lois, but that very same evening he screamed at her for making him wait while she went to the restroom and got caught up in conversation with fans. That was the first outburst Lois had experienced from Frank, but it was enough; they went their separate ways.

Frank continued to support Democratic causes but privately never got over the slight that the Kennedy campaign had inflicted upon him. While he originally mocked Ronald Reagan as an unintelligent, failed actor, he came to support both Reagan's campaign for re-election as governor in 1970 and Nixon's presidential campaigns. This shift was largely due to two factors: the vice president's determined efforts to win Frank over to the campaign and the decision by Frank's Mafia connections that the Republican party was more likely to work in their interests.

Vice President Spiro Agnew reached out to Frank, and the two began spending a lot of time together. Frank was officially invited to the Nixon campaign despite protests that his Mafia connections would create bad publicity for the presidential candidate. Knowing how to cater to Frank's ego, Nixon asked Frank to come out of retirement to sing at his inaugural ball. Frank gladly accepted.

Frank found more loyal friends in the Nixon administration than those of the Kennedy group, and he returned the loyalty when the party ran into trouble. Even when Frank insulted a female reporter at the White House, he was still invited back. Frank helped Vice President Agnew pay for legal costs when he was accused of tax evasion and eventually resigned, and the only comment he made on the Watergate scandal was, "No one's perfect." According to daughter Tina, while Frank may have appeared to switch political alliances, he remained committed to the same Democratic beliefs, including a woman's right to have an abortion and gun control.

Frank's retirement did not last long, as many close to him predicted. Even before Frank's performance at the 1973 inaugural ball, he had sung at private events, including fundraisers and campaign events. Finally, in 1974 Frank began appearing publicly in concerts once again. Under the slogan "Ol' Blue Eyes Is Back," a publicity gimmick coined by Reprise Records—since Frank had never been referred to by that name until then—Frank came back onstage with the hit song "Let Me Try Again." Audiences flocked to see him, but some were disappointed at the older, clearly wigged appearance of their former idol. Others claimed that he was still as stylish as ever.

Frank admitted that he couldn't stand to be away from show business, and he claimed that he had never wanted to retire but, rather, had just wanted a rest. Frank also continued his bad behaviors, including womanizing as well as threatening and injuring journalists and bystanders.

Spiro Agnew in Brief

On November 9, 1918, Spiro Agnew was born to Greek immigrants in Maryland. He lived the American dream, attending college and then law school. After spending some time in the army, marrying and starting a family, and finishing law school, he began his involvement with politics in his home state. He was elected governor of Maryland after a few years serving in smaller political roles.

Agnew went on the ticket with Richard Nixon and became the thirty-ninth vice president of the United States. The Nixon administration encountered its own scandals, and Agnew was no less under fire. He was accused of a variety of crimes that supposedly took place during his time as governor, including bribery and extortion. He ultimately resigned his office in 1973.

Agnew and his wife had four children. He spent his later years working in international business. Agnew died on September 17, 1996, of leukemia.

Chapter 22: Mrs. Barbara Sinatra

When in Palm Springs one day, visiting Frank, in 1960, Ava Gardner had become bored and invited some neighbors to play tennis at a nearby racquet club. The neighbors were Zeppo Marx and his wife, Barbara. Barbara was a former Las Vegas showgirl who had met Marx while performing at a casino and had married him when she was thirty-two and he was fifty-eight. The couple lived near Frank in Palm Springs. Barbara took to visiting Frank and Ava frequently while her older, ailing husband stayed home, even though Ava claimed that Frank detested Barbara.

Fourteen years later, Barbara had divorced from Marx and was seen constantly with Frank. He claimed that she was "the sunshine of his life." At the same time, however, he dated other women and vacationed with his first wife, Nancy. Frank told his daughters that he had hopes of getting back together with their mother Nancy but, soon thereafter, proposed to Barbara.

Barbara and Frank wed on July 11, 1976. Frank's daughters and mother, who did not care for Barbara, attended the wedding, as did Ronald Reagan, Spiro Agnew, and many celebrities. Barbara wasted no time in remodeling Frank's Palm Springs home to her liking. Friends reported that she controlled which of Frank's friends were permitted to visit, and many old cronies of Frank now felt unwelcome there.

Ava Gardner received calls from Frank right up to the wedding, trying to convince Ava to come back to him. Finally, she told Frank to marry Barbara, confiding to a friend that Frank was getting old and needed someone who would stay with him—and Barbara would, but Ava would not. Ava's words proved prophetic as Barbara stayed married to Frank for the next twenty years, until the end of Frank's life.

Frank appeared to benefit from married life. Reports of his drinking and affairs decreased, and he performed at ninety-two concerts during the first nine months of his marriage. He released his famous song "New York, New York" in 1979, and it immediately became a worldwide hit, embodying both that city's great spirit and Frank's own defiant victories. In 1971, at the age of sixty-six, Frank had told a reporter that he would perform until he couldn't do so anymore. He lived up to his word; for the next nearly twenty years, he performed more shows than he had in his whole career up to that point.

Frank's family life witnessed some shake-ups during this time. Barbara, having converted to Catholicism, convinced Frank to have his wedding to Nancy annulled, an act that deeply upset Nancy and Nancy's children, who considered the Church's word sacred. Worse, Dolly died at the age of eighty, not from old age but in a plane crash while taking a flight to Las Vegas to see Frank perform. Frank, who had fought with his mother until the day she died, entered into a stark period of mourning after her loss.

Frank's legal troubles due to his Mob connections did not end with his youth. In 1978, a Mafia-run New York theater was shut down, and eleven defendants were convicted of stock fraud, racketeering, and other offenses related to its operation. Frank had appeared at the theater several times and was pictured in a photograph with eight other men, all mobsters associated with the theater scandal. Frank explained the photo away by claiming that he was merely asked to pose in a picture as a celebrity and did so without knowing the criminal connections of the men who joined him. Those who witnessed Frank's interactions with the men, however, saw Frank greet many of the major mobsters with kisses and hugs, as though they were family. The FBI also had information that another mobster, an admittedly close friend of Frank's named Al Pacella, was now managing the Mob's interest in Frank. Frank was never officially charged with any crime, but his name came up repeatedly in hearings and evidence files.

The well-publicized case did not prevent President Ronald Reagan from asking Frank to direct his inaugural gala. Telling the papers that he simply hoped the things he was hearing about Frank weren't true, he continued to welcome Frank into the White House. The gala raised millions of dollars. Shortly thereafter, Frank applied for a new gambling license from the Nevada gambling authority. He put down Reagan's name as a reference, and Reagan told the board that Frank was honest and loyal. Frank was granted the license despite being unable to explain various associations with mobsters.

Frank continued to raise money for Reagan, and Reagan asked him to organize his second inaugural gala. In 1985 Reagan awarded Frank the Medal of Freedom, the highest award available to a civilian, for his humanitarian and civil rights work.

In 1986, when Frank was about to turn seventy-one, author Kitty Kelly published a best-selling biography on Frank Sinatra entitled *His Way*. Frank had known of its preparation and had tried to sue Kelley to stop its publication. Frank's litigious acts had the opposite of the intended effect and flamed the book's popularity when it finally was published. The book contained information about Frank's dealings with the Mafia, his predilection for prostitutes, and his violent behavior. Frank's family was extremely embarrassed by the book, and Frank refused to acknowledge its existence.

Zeppo Marx in Brief

Herbert Manfred Marx was born on February 25, 1901. The source of his nickname is up for debate. Some anecdotes claim it refers to zeppelins, others to Mr. Zippo the chimpanzee, a popular act in Zeppo's younger days.

He appeared with his famous older brothers, Groucho, Gummo, Harpo, and Chico, in five films. The Marx brothers enjoyed a long run as America's favorite funny family. Zeppo, the youngest, often served as the straight man for his zany brothers, although most reports indicate that he was very funny but was forced into the more serious, romantic roles because of his good looks and youth.

After leaving the brotherly comedy troupe, Zeppo had a variety of careers. He was well known for his knack with machines, in particular. His marriage to Barbara was his second.

On November 30, 1979 Zeppo died of cancer. He was the last surviving Marx brother.

Chapter 23: Frank Sinatra, Still Performing

Frank seemed to be determined to perform until he literally could not do so anymore. Despite medical problems, including an operation on polyps in his colon and a painful intestinal abscess, Frank performed in sixty-eight concerts in 1987. He convinced Dean Martin and Sammy Davis Jr. to go on a "Together Again" tour to twenty-nine cities. All three men were advanced in age, and Dean Martin especially was suffering from the physical effects of years of alcohol abuse. Martin withdrew from the tour after a short while, too exhausted to party with Frank into the night. Liza Minnelli replaced Martin.

Frank began to lose his friends to death. In 1986 Ava suffered a stroke that left her partially paralyzed. Now living in London, she began writing a biography with author Peter Evans. As her health continued to fail, Frank sent a plane to bring her to California for medical treatment. While in California, Ava was ferried to the hospital daily in a limousine commissioned by Frank. Ava died in 1987, shortly after her sixty-seventh birthday. Frank did not attend the funeral, but attendees at a concert that he gave the day after witnessed him staggering around the stage in a fog, drinking heavily, and appearing to remember Ava as he sang "One for My Baby." Sammy Davis Jr. died of throat cancer in 1990. Frank was also devastated by this loss. Then Dean Martin died on Christmas Day of 1995.

In 1991, at the age of seventy-five, Frank began a world tour. He played eighty or more concerts that year and each of the following two years, then sixty concerts in 1994. Despite his addiction to show business, Frank's age was beginning to take its toll. Alarmingly, he forgot the words to well-known songs. Friends witnessed him rambling incoherently at times, likely due to the fact that Frank continued to drink heavily even while his mind showed early signs of dementia, and he took prescription medications.

Frank worried about his finances, and for good cause: despite his riches, Frank had overspent for several years, and part of the reason that he had come out of retirement was to save himself from financial ruin. Frank's voice was no longer the force that it once was, but he still performed with his trademark style and innovation, and could still captivate audiences with his stories and experimental twists on old favorites.

Inside the family, strife was brewing. Frank's daughters Tina and Nancy fought with Barbara over their father's medications and the rescission of a premarital agreement. They claimed that Barbara put on a front of being a caring, devoted wife but that, when no visitors were around, she treated Frank dismissively and unkindly. They believed firmly that Barbara had married Frank for his money.

In 1992 Frank's longtime friend Jilly Rizzo was killed in a car accident. Frank, although despairing, continued his planned European tour. That fall, he performed with Shirley MacLaine on a tour of nine American cities. In 1993 he re-entered the recording studio at the urging of record producer Phil Ramone, who arranged for Frank to sing digitally coordinated duets with other huge stars including Barbra Streisand, Aretha Franklin, Luther Vandross, and Bono. Although hesitant, Frank performed solo and listened in amazement as his voice was digitally merged with others'. The *Duets* album, released in October of 1993, went to the top of the charts and sold millions of records.

In March 1994, Frank was awarded a Grammy "Legend" award, which was presented to him by Bono. Soon after, Frank seemed to sink even further into old age, collapsing on stage in Virginia and losing track of where he was while drinking on the way back from a performance in Tokyo. Frank's last performance was at a Palm Springs hotel, at a golf tournament named after him. On his eightieth birthday, in December 1995, the Empire State Building was lit blue in his honor, and Frank appeared on a two-hour television special—his last.

Frank was the last remaining of many performers of his generation. The Sands Hotel, his old stomping grounds, was closed forever; and Barbara moved Frank out of his Palm

Springs house to their home in the LA area, reportedly to be closer to medical treatment. Much of the memorabilia that marked Frank's career was auctioned off. Frank had agreed to move, but friends reported that he was devastated at the loss of his Palm Springs home. In July 1996, on the twentieth anniversary of their marriage, Frank and Barbara renewed their wedding vows. Frank's children did not attend; they were now in open warfare with Barbara. The papers spoke of the battles between Frank's daughter Tina and Barbara about merchandising and licensing of Frank's image.

Chapter 24: Death and Funeral

In November 1996, Frank had his first heart attack. It was now clear that he had dementia. He retreated to his home, watching TV and drinking with friends. Frank began discussing the possibility of an afterlife with friends, including Shirley MacLaine. On the evening of May 14, 1998, Frank suffered a second, much more severe heart attack. Barbara was out to dinner with friends at the time. He was rushed to Cedars-Sinai Hospital, suffered another heart attack, and was pronounced dead at 10:50 p.m. Barbara arrived to the hospital while the doctors were working on him, and his two daughters shortly after his death. They had not been alerted immediately.

Frank was the last of many performers of his generation. At Frank's memorial service in Hoboken, New Jersey, the church where Frank was baptized was filled to capacity. In Las Vegas, another tribute was paid: the casinos on the strip turned off their lights for a couple of minutes while people gathered on the streets outside, holding candles. In New York, the top of the Empire State Building was lit blue. The official funeral mass, held in a church in Beverly Hills, was attended by many famous people as well as all of Frank's living wives: Nancy Barbato, Mia Farrow, and Barbara Sinatra. At the end of the service, Frank's song "Put Your Dreams Away" was played. Frank was buried in Desert Memorial Park, California. Frank's gravestone read, "The Best Is Yet to Come."

Afterword

Biographers have struggled to explain what exactly about Frank Sinatra made him a legend. After all, there were many stylish, hard-drinking, lavish-living artists in his day. Most agree that Frank Sinatra's fame and legacy came from his ability to reach audiences, to reach across time and space with the power of his voice as thousands of people yearned for that connection. Frank Sinatra, by being the Voice of the Lonely, touched millions of listeners over several decades that changed America drastically, and he connected with them in a real way. That is why his name and his music live on.

Please enjoy a free chapter of Houdini: A Life Worth Reading, also available from Higher Read.

III. Houdini, the King of Handcuffs

Houdini arrived in London believing that bookings were waiting for him. He was enraged to find out that the international agent that Beck referred him to had failed to have anything ready. Houdini set out to drum up publicity by challenging the Scotland Yard police to confine him. He managed to get himself booked at the famous London theatre the Alhambra. London audiences loved his act, and Houdini quickly became famous there. However, he had to work harder to spread his fame into the English countryside, as the managers of theaters at various villages felt that his magic act did not fit what the family audiences of the time wanted. Houdini doggedly performed auditions for managers, until word of his unique tricks spread and he became a headliner in the country villages as well. He also advertised himself by performing the Nude Cell Escape at police stations in the small villages of the countryside. In one particularly famous performance in Sheffield, Houdini escaped from the high security unit where one of London's most famous murderers, Charles Pace, had been imprisoned.

For Houdini's onstage performances, he wore the formal dress of the time: a stiff, high collar, a white dickey, and a black dress coat. Bess frequently assisted him, wearing black knickerbockers. Houdini's brother Dash sometimes assisted as well or instead. Frequently there was a physician contracted to be backstage or onstage in case of emergency. Houdini performed his handcuff escapes behind a curtain, over which the audience could sometimes see his head, or else in a "cabinet" or "ghost house," a construction made to conceal Houdini's techniques from the audience.

Houdini's stage manner was something he studied and practiced almost as much as his magic. He worked hard to engage the audience and win them over to his side, presenting tricks with careful showmanship. He frequently made jokes that seemed self-deprecating, while also carefully building the tension in his audience members to keep them spellbound. He involved the audience in every way possible, an original tactic at the time.

In 1901 Houdini arranged with Beck to be let out of his contract. He became his own manager. In 1902, he introduced a new trick: the Packing Case Escape. A packing case was essentially a large crate that merchants of the time used for shipping. This act was a twist on the Metamorphosis trick. Houdini would arrange for a local store to provide the crate, and then would have assistants nail him into the crate onstage. Inspectors selected from the audience would verify its complete closing. The secret to Houdini's escape involved his ability to noiselessly disassemble the crate from the inside; Bess or another ally would direct the nailing shut of the crate such that one wall of the crate was less enforced. Many nails would be hammered into the top of the crate, creating the impression that it was sealed very tight all around. But, since Houdini did not come out of the top of the crate, this did not affect his ability to escape. Audiences loved this trick, and in one particular performance in Glasgow, Scotland at the Zoo-Hippodrome theatre, the crowd filled the theater and the streets outside to see it.

As part of his publicity campaign, Houdini frequently offered a reward to the public to anyone who could cuff him so that he could not escape. He did specify that he would only be cuffed by regulation, unaltered equipment. One experience that haunted him occurred in the working-class city of Blackburn, England. There, a young body-builder by the name of Hodgson challenged him to escape from powerful cuffs with which he had tampered. Goaded by the young man's scorn, Houdini accepted the challenge despite the tampering. Hodgson, who was knowledgeable about anatomy, cuffed Houdini in a torturous way that cut off his circulation and caused great pain. After fifteen minutes of working on the cuffs, Houdini explained that his circulation had been cut off and asked Hodgson to allow him a break from the cuffs for it to return. Hodgson refused. Houdini returned to the torturous struggle, and after almost two hours, emerged free from restraints, his body bloody and torn.

Hodgson, however, scorned Houdini's efforts in a public interview shortly after the performance, saying that he had evidence that Houdini had cut himself out of the cuffs with the help of Bess and his brother Dash, who were onstage with him. Enraged, Houdini changed his plans so that he could return to Blackburn to rebut these charges. Even though he returned to Blackburn on later tours, he always faced Hodgson-supporters who booed him while onstage and challengers that tried to defeat him using damaged cuffs.

In perhaps one of his most-talked-about escapes, a representative from the *London Daily Mirror*, a popular newspaper, came onstage during one of Houdini's performances and told him of a famous pair of handcuffs made by a British blacksmith. The handcuffs had taken the blacksmith five years to make, and were probably the most sophisticated restraints in existence at the time. Only one person, a famous lock-picker, had ever been able to open the cuffs, a feat that took him forty-four hours. Houdini accepted the challenge to escape from these cuffs, and the event was scheduled to take place four days later at a major London theater called the Hippodrome.

When the night finally arrived, the Hippodrome was packed. Houdini explained that he wasn't sure if he was going to be able to open the cuffs, but that he would try his best. He disappeared behind the curtain, appearing once after twenty-two minutes to look at the cuffs in a better light and again after another thirteen minutes to ask for a glass of water. The house manager gave Houdini a cushion to sit on because Houdini reported that his knees were hurting. Houdini disappeared back behind the curtain. After an hour of working on the cuffs, he came out from behind the curtain, looking so disheveled and exhausted that some say that Bess became overwhelmed with emotion and had to leave the theater. He asked to be unlocked just to take off his coat, as he was perspiring heavily. The *Mirror* representative refused to uncuff him unless he admitted defeat. Frustrated and defiant, Houdini managed to get a penknife out of his shirt pocket with his mouth, which he used to cut the coat to shreds, removing it. The audience went crazy. Ten minutes later, Houdini emerged from behind the curtain, uncuffed.

Modern magicians and biographers believe that Houdini must have arranged this trick in collaboration with the *Daily Mirror* in order to gain publicity for both. Lock experts say that there is no way that the cuffs could have been opened without a key, and that Bess must have brought one to Houdini in the glass of water, or else it was put in the cushion that was given to him. Many believe that Houdini designed the famous cuffs himself, and simply waited an hour behind the curtain, coming out to demand water and to cut himself out of the coat for effect. In any case, the performance made Houdini the talk of London for a long time, and Houdini fanned the flame of this publicity by offering one hundred guineas to anyone who could escape the same handcuffs. One young man with exceptionally small hands who could have maneuvered out of the cuffs accepted this challenge, but was stumped when Houdini simply asked him to open the cuffs without being cuffed. By the end of his time at the Hippodrome, worn down from excitement and work, Houdini became ill with a cold that had him in bed for twelve days.

Printed in Great Britain
by Amazon.co.uk, Ltd.,
Marston Gate.